Dirt Poor And L

Unplugging, Downsizing, Going
a New Life

By Kate Singh

Author of *The Frugal Life* and *A Sweet Life in Homemaking*

Edited by Perla Thornwood

Cover by Kate Singh

Find me on YouTube at **Coffee With Kate**

Copyright © 2022 Kate Singh

All rights reserved. No portion of this book may be reproduced in any form without permission from the publisher, except as permitted by U.S. copyright law. For permissions contact: Kate Singh via email: vondola@yahoo.com

Table of Contents

Chapter 1

Making Life Changes and Living on Smaller Budgets

Chapter 2

Don't Be Afraid to Be a Little Broke to Follow a Dream

Chapter 3

How to Recreate a World That Supports Your Dreams

Chapter 4

Be Broke for the Time Being and Focus on Creating

Chapter 5

How I Prepared to Work Less

Chapter 6

Movies That Have Inspired Change

Chapter 7

Making a Home Sanctuary and Zen-like Living

Chapter 8

Daily Life In The "Other" World

Chapter 9

Routines and Rituals for Mental Well-Being

Chapter 10

A New Way of Spending Money or Thinking About It

Chapter 11

A Normal Day for Unplugged Folk

Chapter 1

Making Life Changes and Living on Smaller Budgets

The other day, I watched a Studio Ghibli movie called *Only Yesterday*, about a woman who spends her summer vacation working on a farm in the country. We follow her reflections of her fifth-grade self and all the pivotal moments that shaped her and her life. I won't go into the whole movie, but it is a lovely journey to go on, and in the end, she has a choice to make: go back to her lackluster job in the city or stay in the beautiful countryside doing work she loves and staying with people who adore her.

It seems that many people are exploring this today. It's rumored that people are quitting their jobs and taking different paths by the masses; that large numbers of people are questioning their priorities and searching for something more soulful.

I know I was. I recently made some big changes, and what a fantastic decision it was to have done so. Life is unfolding in magical ways. Of course, there are dips, but I won't even look back. There is nothing more exciting than taking a leap into the unknown with so many possibilities ahead. But sometimes, taking said leap requires a budget. We will explore many things here, including soul searching, reducing the budget in order to afford to soul-search, and the question of whether or not this is all worth it in the end. I will tell you now that yes, it is worth it. But can you afford it? That will be for you to figure out as I couldn't possibly know everyone's personal situation. I will just share mine and how it is we make it happen.

I strongly believe in signs. I don't believe in coincidence or luck. I don't ignore a thing. Source is always communicating with our inner selves and we have guidance right there for us if we just pay attention and shut off the monkey mind. We are being guided, protected, and provided for all the time. The Universe and all it has to offer is always surrounding us, waiting to serve. However, we are usually too busy in our overbooked, scheduled lives to take any notice, thus we wind up on the wrong path. We end up going the wrong way, heading toward trouble, and away from our destinies.

I've been rereading *Essentialism* by Greg McKeown lately. The book seems to be more for the corporate world, to help the managers and CEOs figure out the unnecessary so they can lead their team to success. But if this works for talented, brilliant minds to run forward-thinking companies in ways that ensure they thrive, I decided it would do wonders for my humble life at home. I applied this technique to every nook and cranny of my life, our lives as a family, and how I run the house and my many side jobs.

When I first read this book, I spent nights staring at the ceiling, going back in time, reflecting on prior years when I had felt peaceful, and life was slow and quiet. I reflected on people from my past and how they lived their lives simply or had done something to change their lives completely.

In the book, McKeown talks about trade-offs. He talks about how a priority is singular, but we've made it plural with long lists of priorities instead of a couple of choices. Trade-offs are what we trade for something better in the long run.

Since the day this book came into my life, I've been contemplating what I would be willing to trade and what the goal is. I was in a real predicament with overworking and burnout. I was publishing books and blogging almost daily. I had a YouTube channel and a Patreon account. At that time, we were fixing up our second old house and trying to be foster parents. It was all too much.

I began weeding out jobs that were taking too much time and not giving much satisfaction. I began slowing down here and there. I knew the only way I could truly slow down was to reduce our costs back to one income, but we were accustomed to a few sources of income at this point. Adjusting down is never easy.

The entire process took over a year because I was *afraid* we couldn't make it on one income, and I was *afraid* to let go of my social media and not have a way to promote my books. I was *afraid* of disconnecting and being forgotten. There was an ingrained habit as well. I had been writing blog posts and making YouTube videos for years, and it was as common a daily routine as brushing my teeth and drinking coffee in the morning. I filmed, wrote, and edited daily. So we had fear and a deep-rooted habit of overworking at play.

Fast forward to today. For a list of reasons, I decided to pause the Internet in our house. After a week or so I saw incredibly positive changes with my family. I called up Xfinity and canceled it altogether. I then canceled many other things until we had a bare-bones budget and could once again live under one income. That hadn't happened in years.

Early in my marriage and when our boys were babes, we lived on a small, tight budget. I was much happier then. I didn't blog, write, nor film. I nested and tended to little children. I spent my days vacuuming, watching over babies in our backyard while reading Amish fiction and *The Tightwad Gazette* by Amy Dacyczyn. I loved Cathy Mitchell's *Dump Dinners* cookbook and made simple casseroles and baked brownies or store-bought blackberry cobblers. At night, we listened to coyotes hunting in the orchards, and in the morning, we woke with the sun and freshly brewed coffee. Life was slow and quiet.

I would have friends from far away come stay with us every six months to a year. My neighbor would sit with me under a tree in a grassy area between the houses and we would drink O'Doul's and chat. I had a high school girlfriend that came back into my life since we lived near each other again, and she would come out once a week and visit. She and I would make big buckets of homemade laundry detergent and spend time together. She introduced me to WinCo Foods. She called it bin heaven because of all the bulk bins filled with everything from pasta, nuts, herbs, and candy, to dog food and birdseed. It is employee-owned, and they cut out the middleman, therefore making their prices the best around.

I read all the time back then. A friend had given me a few books that included Amish fiction and I was hooked. We had a tiny library in our small town of 700 people, and the librarian there showed me how to go online and order books from all over the place, including other towns and even other counties. My husband Bali would bring home bags and bags of Amish fiction books that I had previously ordered, and I would devour them between changing diapers, nursing, and making one-pot dishes.

I was never online in those days. I didn't understand what YouTube was and I detested Facebook. I listened to the radio or put on Disney music and nursery rhymes for the boys and read them stacks of children's books right along with my novels. That was our sweet life.

We had a small budget, and I used a grocery envelope out of necessity. We had no wiggle room. Bali worked long hours for a small paycheck. I didn't mess around. I was very careful with every dollar, and I read everything I could find on being frugal, even being somewhat cheap.

We lived well and ate well and wanted for nothing. But I never shopped frivolously or ordered things online. I don't remember buying much besides the used edition of *The Complete Tightwad Gazette* and *Dump Dinners*. We had everything we could need or want. I stocked up on baby clothes from thrift stores and I had a room full of toys from a daycare business I previously had. If I needed something, I found it on Craigslist or at the thrift store.

I've been thinking about those days fondly. It is nostalgic and reminds me of a time when we didn't need much money.

You might think our rent was cheaper back then, but it wasn't. It was $1,300 per month and today our mortgage payment is $1,330. The fact that I recently had so much trouble getting our budget down was perplexing, to say the least. I figured out that we had become comfortable on a larger income with my royalties and I was a spender. Not a frivolous spender, but a spender, nonetheless. We always needed something for the house, the garden, the kitchen, the yard...

It is a hole that can never be filled up with stuff. You must cut yourself off as you would with any bad habit. I think quitting sugar recently helped me confront a problem head-on and make the change. I also started eating in a timed window, also known as intermittent fasting. I eat from 8 a.m. to 4 p.m. or 7 a.m. to 3 p.m., depending on when I have my first cup of coffee. It has helped my energy levels and I feel rather good so far. I fail often but each day is another chance, right?!

Around this time, I began asking myself what was most important in our lives and where I wanted to channel my energy. The Internet was gone. I was releasing the last of the items that held us back.

I've talked about my friend, Miss B in previous books as well as my YouTube channel and people love hearing her story. She used to live on government assistance and later, disability. Unfortunately, she passed away from an autoimmune disease several years ago. She lived on so little and still managed to have a cozy and clean home as well as put food on the table for her and her children. Many people struggle on very little, and they want the magic formula. There isn't one, but it can be done.

I learned a lot from Miss B before she left this life. To this day, I try to use her advice on cozy homemaking and frugality. If anyone knew how to live on a penny, it was her.

But the one person I remember who inspires me in a big way today was Miss B's neighbor from thirty years ago. I was in my early twenties and lived with Miss B for a couple of months before moving back to the city. Back then, she was a single mother of one child and working as an aid to an elderly lady. She lived in some very plain apartments with no landscaping. They were just rows of long, stacked, tan buildings with no character.

Miss B's neighbor, who I call Miss D, lived across the way and above the parking garage. She went to college full-time. She was an older woman, newly divorced, with two daughters who were just starting high school. She realized that her choices were to either work all the time and scrap by, and never be around for her girls, *or* go back to college full-time. She chose college. She devoted her life 100% to being there for her daughters during the awkward teenage years and supporting them through the big emotions of dealing with a broken family. She was there for all their school and sporting events, she was home when they got home from school, she was baking brownies for the school bake sales, and she did everything with them. She also gave her all to her education at the local community college, which was all she could afford to attend. It was close by, and all her schooling was paid for with BOG fee waivers and financial aid. Fortunately, this college offered everything, and she took almost a double load every semester.

A full school load was 12 units, and she took 16 to 20 units each semester. I would visit her sometimes and the table would be piled high with textbooks, papers, and an old, humming computer. She was always brewing coffee and studying or writing papers.

The trade-off was that she went on government aid. I don't know how much or if she received child support, but she lived on pennies. Her car was an old beat-up rig that kept getting her to college and back, but she didn't travel far with it. I remember going to the food bank with her once and that was back when food banks were not as supported by local stores and farmer donations. It was government cheese blocks and bags of government beans and rice. She was very careful with every dollar she had, so she and her daughters never went out, never ate out, and she only shopped for groceries from the most inexpensive stores she could find.

The payoff was that she was there for her girls during the tough years, and they turned out well. I know this because Miss B stayed friends with her for decades and I would hear about her now and then. I know that Miss D earned two or three degrees from the community college, wound up running one of the departments, and retired from that very college. She bought a sweet little cottage and was able to support her daughters.

So, it isn't a sacrifice when there is a big, wonderful goal. We do make trade-offs and to some, living a broke life may seem depressing. Surprisingly, it has many hidden gems.

A broke life often looks more like a very stripped-down, simple life. It is humble and a lot of creativity is needed to live well when money is not abundant.

Chapter 2

Don't Be Afraid to Be a Little Broke to Follow a Dream

What is your reason for changing to a more frugal life? There are many reasons, but what about having more freedom, more time, and more creative space? How about just having more time with family? Or like Miss D, obtaining an education or making a career change?

I was burned out but kept going and adding more and more hustles. At first, it was because we had a huge goal to move to a different town. Then, I think it just became a bad habit and we got used to living on more income (the usual trap), and I liked to spend money and shop. I had become quite the online shopper.

I had so many money hustles going but I wasn't doing any of them well and I wasn't running our home or raising my family in a stellar way. I was spreading myself thin. Greg McKeown talks of having many priorities and our energy going all over the place but not making much progress. If we choose one or two priorities our energy is concentrated in a small space, and we thrive.

Over the year, I began some soul searching and letting go of this hustle and that side job. As I let go of jobs, the other parts of our life began to improve, but I still had one job too many and I found that the Internet was devouring hours of my day. My children were losing their childhood to Minecraft, other games, and silly YouTube videos.

I began to think of another book that had a big impact on my vision of living: *What Falls From The Sky*, by Esther Emery. It is about her year off the Internet completely, and I mean completely. She used cash and paper maps and tried writing about her experience on paper to send to a friend to post on her blog for her. She even gave up documenting the experience when her sister confronted her about really giving herself to the process.

For Esther, it was a year of healing. Her marriage was falling apart, her life was going a thousand miles an hour, and she was a mess. So she and her family moved to a new town, and she took the year to stay home and focus on family and her mental well-being. She is the daughter of Carla Emery, author of *The Encyclopedia of Country Living*. Carla was famous for homesteading and homemaking from scratch. Esther detested all of it. She was also a proclaimed atheist. However, as the year went on, she found a church and began a new relationship with God, took to homemaking and cooking, and healed deeply. She and her family wound up moving to the mountains and doing off-grid homesteading. You can find her channels, *Fouch Family Off Grid* and *Esther Emery*, on YouTube. You can find her book at the library. I've reordered that book as well since it seems to take me several seasons to truly "get" a thing.

A year or so later, I have called it quits with our Internet. I grew up in the '70s and '80s. As a kid, we had a huge antenna on the roof that, if my mother got up there and moved around, might get us two or three channels. I grew up when the first computers were big, tan boxes that sat heavily on one's desk and had ugly green letters on a black screen. We had a phone attached to the wall and had to dial numbers found in a paper address book. I still remember our number from when I was 15 years old because we had to punch it in vigorously every time. I would call my mother from payphones inside Round Table Pizza if I wanted to come home.

I didn't get my first computer until I was 31 and I probably had a flip phone years later - I can't remember. I was way behind, and I fought technology and its encroachment for as long as I could get away with it. I was the last person on the jogging trails to carry a fanny pack with cassette tapes for my Walkman. I remember changing out a self-recorded tape on this Walkman and catching a couple of people laughing at me from afar. I soon switched to the Discman which I also clung to far past its "cool" phase.

Now here I am with a YouTube channel, and I've had all the social media you can name: Twitter, LinkedIn, Facebook, Instagram...and I detested them all. Years ago, I got rid of these social media outlets but kept my YouTube channel. I never felt better the day I deleted my Facebook account and all the others as well. I felt free and never looked back.

However, I recently found us rotting away on the laptops so I decided to put the Internet on pause for six months in the new year. After a couple of weeks, the transformation in the family was so delightful that I called up Xfinity and asked them to cancel our contract permanently. I got rid of the home phone that we had kept for 10 years because it was through our Internet. I don't regret it at all. Unfortunately, now I've cleverly figured out how to work the data on my cell phone so that must go next. I'm purposely making it hard to be online because I have seen a huge decline in my reading and book writing since becoming immersed.

My kids were always allowed to watch PBS cartoons or do some ABCMouse, but the Internet was off-limits, and they were never to touch our phones. Since those rules changed and I got them Minecraft, their interest in playing outdoors, playdates, parks, bikes at the fairgrounds, even building with toys was no longer of interest.

I used to write prolifically, both fiction and nonfiction. I used to read stacks of books of all genres and authors. Now I waste hours watching mind-sucking videos on how to make 140 recipes on $50 or "clean with me" videos that I drink coffee to while I cheer them on but don't often inspire me to do much more than the dishes.

Since cutting off the Internet, my boys are spending most hours outside and there are, much to my joy and irritation, toys all over the house that are once again in business. I can't wait to do my chores and rest with another cup of coffee to read my books. We socialize, have our old playdates, and I thumb through my cookbooks at the kitchen table. We are coming back to life.

It is hard to live a simple life these days. There are laptops and iPhones and tablets everywhere you look, and the Internet seems to be eating up our lives. We have internet IVs hooked up to our brains and social media has replaced real life. To be offline is archaic and preposterous to some. I had a few people on my channel claim they didn't believe me that we were offline as if this was such a huge and wild jump. A friend gave me four months as if I'm attempting to train for a triathlon.

Now, to be clear, we do go to the library to get our fix or to get work done. I do have data on my phone, and I am now using my cell phone far more often. It is how bad habits go. They find a way to survive. Soon we will be switching to Mint Mobile to save money and I have chosen to NOT have data with that plan because apparently I'm a child who needs the candy to just *not* be there to tempt me. I'm being honest.

Now what? Social media deleted, Internet off...

Soul searching continues and it turns out I'm still too busy. More in my head than hands. Busy in hands work too but the mind is spinning around all the time. I'm fascinated with the Buddhist and Zen monks, and I watched little clips on how they live. I have no desire to be a monk but that quiet life of sweeping the courtyard after a morning of meditation and eating a bowl of rice and bland broth. Ah, what a peaceful existence.

There is a wonderful documentary called *How To Cook Your Life* with Zen chef Edward Espe Brown. It used to be free on VUDU, but it must have become popular because you now have to rent it. Well worth the $3.99. I just purchased it with the last of my Amazon gift card for $3.00 because I cannot tell you how much this documentary on food and our inner lives has made another huge impact on me. I must have watched it 20 times, playing it in the background just to absorb the energy of it.

Edward teaches his students to bake and talks about how our food has gone from mothers' pantries to factory foods and the effect that has on the environment as well as on our spiritual well-being. I completely agree. The more I cook from scratch the cleaner our food is and the cozier my kitchen becomes with the bowls of dough rising, granola baking slowly in the oven, and homemade sauces simmering on the stove. The smells of cooking fill the house and each dish has some semblance of nutrition for all souls in this house. The side effects are a healthier family, a lot of money saved, and more feasting around the kitchen table.

Reducing the Income: The Preparation

There are many ways I began preparing to reduce our income and simplify our life. But first, let's talk about why I have this craving to do so.

I'm an older mother. I got married the summer before I turned 41. I had my first son at 41 and my second and last son at 43. I hadn't planned this, it's just how life happened. I was sure I was headed for spinsterhood and an empty nest. I would work to the bitter end at some job serving up soup or typing up forms. I had skills in the office and café, so that was good.

Fate was kind and swooped in at the last minute and I was blessed with a family and took up my position at home. For some, this is a boring job filled with drudgery and loneliness. I read something like that in *The Have-More*

Plan toward the back of the book when the woman tries to encourage other housewives to simplify and enjoy their housework. I never felt that way. I couldn't wait to tend to my own home and take care of a family. I love nesting. To me, it is like having a grown-up dollhouse. I have overused this example, but it is just like that as I decorate and switch out curtains or rearrange the furniture in every room. I find colorful area rugs, paintings, lamps, and even furniture at thrift stores. I used to only shop at thrift stores and/or Craigslist back in the day when I was very prudent and taking care of my husband's money.

I have always wanted this career as a housewife, and I was thrilled the day my last office job threw me a going-away party. I knew the next day I would begin my new life at home, and I took it up with both hands. I was pretty good from the start, but I have improved vastly over the last decade. So much has been learned since those early days.

The biggest skill I learned was how to be frugal with a small paycheck. I learned this early on when my husband's workplace went out of business, and we had no income for some months. I quickly obtained a license and built a small daycare that I ran for a short time until we moved to another town far from my beloved ocean. Bali found a job making $10.68 an hour and had to work a lot. We rented the cheapest place we could find that would take dogs. Dogs are a gift but when hard times hit, having them complicates things a bit. We moved to a tiny town on the river in farmland and there were two places for rent. One was a scam, I'm pretty sure, so we had one option, and thank goodness it was a wonderful place. The managers of the property were very welcoming and even built us a fence around the backyard to keep the dogs and boys from running off. Our rent was reasonable and looking back, it was fantastic for what we enjoyed.

But we made very little, and I'd say almost 50% went to rent. I dove into learning everything I could about stretching a small income over a month. I had already learned how to pay off debt from prior experience and I had learned small tricks such as using cash envelopes and finding affordable groceries at discount markets. I had café skills, house cleaning skills, and office/managerial skills from over two decades of being out in the workforce. I used all my skills to run the house and manage our money.

I learned to order everything from the library, and I researched like crazy. I bought *The Complete Tightwad Gazette*, then I ordered stacks of free books from the library on frugality, cheapskate living, thrifting, and stories about families living on very little.

I had Miss B back then. She and I had known each other since we were 15 years old and were in and out of each other's lives for years. She got married and had her first daughter at a very young age. I remember she lived in a tiny rental and cooked a lot of instant rice and cheap cuts of chicken. She kept her little house clean and neat and took pride in her motherhood and homemaking. Down the road, she got divorced and was a single mother. She worked and struggled. That was about the time I stayed with her for a couple of months when I was in my twenties.

In later years, Miss B remarried, worked hard, had another child and added stepchildren, and ran a daycare for years. Sadly, life doesn't always end well, and she divorced and wound up injured from a job and on government assistance. In her last years, she suffered from an autoimmune disease that seemed to have kicked in shortly after a very invasive weight loss surgery, and she went on disability. She passed away in her 40s, days before I had Sam, my youngest son. She had a hard life. But what I like to remember about her is that she was a wonderful homemaker until the end. She tried to teach me things on saving money and getting by on a tight budget for when I became a housewife, but quite frankly I had lost hope of that happening and ignored most of what she said. When I did marry and have children and we lived on less than $2,800 a month, I listened carefully and recalled much of how she lived.

To be honest, I didn't realize how poor she was when I visited her in my single years. Her house was old and worn, but so clean, and she used tablecloths to cover ugly tables, afghans to cover old couches, and she always had a candle or two lit - one on the table and one on a side table by her recliner. She always had food and there was either a big container of sun brewed iced tea or steamy hot coffee brewing. Christmas was a big deal to her. She always had a brightly decorated tree along with gifts for everyone, fully stuffed stockings, and there was always a table spread with homemade fudge or sugar cookies. She also liked to serve cheap Brie cheese she found at Grocery Outlet that she baked with crescent roll dough, or her cheapest and most fabulous trick of baked garlic with sourdough - all found on sale or deeply discounted. She always had two turkeys in the chest freezer in the garage and she would start collecting stocking stuffers and baking ingredients right after Christmas and would collect all year.

As some know from present or past experience when on government assistance or disability, you have no wiggle room. You must make a small amount last all month. She did have help from her parents and the church, but she also found a way to stretch the money. She was the type to go to FoodMaxx with $50 and come out with bags of groceries. She wasn't that health-conscious, that is true, but her cupboards were full, and everyone was fed.

She always dressed nicely, even when she was at her heaviest. She wore $0.25 T-shirts and shorts, or Capri stretch pants. They were clean and had no stains or holes. She wore sneakers or flip-flops purchased cheaply at drugstores. This was a simple outfit, but she dolled it up with big earrings and a full face of makeup (she loved her makeup, and she had a lovely face for it). She clipped her curly hair up and always wore inexpensive but nicely smelling scented lotions she found cheaply at a hospice thrift store. Her toenails were always painted when she wore flip flops. She found almost everything at this hospice thrift store with the best prices. She would never step foot in a Goodwill, saying they were far too expensive. She found clothes, scented candles, lotions and such for less than a dollar. I remember going to a church flea market with her once, and they were charging $1 for everything you could fit in a bag. She had the time to hunt and peck and find the deals. And she did.

I have been thinking of Miss B and Miss D recently because I have decided to create a small budget as we had so many years ago when I made no money. I feel called to simplify our lives and withdraw from the frenetic world at this time. I feel moved to be more present with my boys and life in general. Be here now, that is the mantra.

Get rid of the stress, the hustles. Get rid of money worries and focus on the delights of life - on children, baking in a sunny kitchen, connecting with others on a deeper and more meaningful level, and going on long walks.

I watched *The Illusion Of Money* with Kyle Cease last night. It is about our fears of poverty or being broke and how being driven by this fear often keeps us in stifling jobs or feeling trapped in life due to money issues. But what if we let go of that fear and said, "Oh well, so I'll be broke for some time"? It releases that worry, and we can find what brings us joy and create, play, build, and make things.

I'd like to go back to a time when I didn't work around the clock, and I felt calm and loving all the time. When I began my writing career, I typed away on my $300 laptop Bali purchased for me during one of our trips to Costco. I read fat novels from the library, and I thought about books and writing, stories, endings, beginnings, fiction, and nonfiction. I also had a tread climber at the time, and I walked on it for an hour every day. I read or listened to music and thought about what I was writing while getting my miles in.

Besides the insecurities of those early years with my writing, it was a soulful time. I was more productive and filled with rich ideas and creative thoughts in a short span of two years than ever before. I have written several more books over the years since then and my homemaking books kept improving, but my fiction faded away with only one book in five years, whereas I wrote four fictional books in the first two years. What happened to lose that imagination and ability to write fiction?

Well, I started blogging on homemaking, then we bought a house, and I became consumed with homesteading in town, then I started a YouTube channel about homemaking. This is not a bad thing. I have been creating wonderful things and learning so much about the craft of homemaking, gardening, cooking from scratch, and so on. I have been sharing it in all forms. But the other side of my personality that I also enjoy and cherish has been shoved in a box and put up on a shelf in a closet somewhere. I can't seem to access it.

I also have boys who love to talk and make noise all day. I have chores, dogs that need exercise, one of which is elderly now, meals to cook, and a husband that comes home tired and hungry.

Where is the creative space? No wonder the fictional life has faded.

So, I read and reread *Essentialism*. I read *What Falls From The Sky*. I thought about my future. I read my old bumper sticker on our Toyota Corolla the other day: "*Remember What You Wanted To Be When You Grew Up?*" A writer. Creative and fun. I wanted to write books people could get lost in.

Thus, my journey back to my dream begins.

Chapter 3

How to Recreate a World That Supports Your Dreams

While typing this work, I did find Miss D. I had been trying to find her for some time, so it was very strange that I picked up my cell phone and found her so easily. I remembered her last name from a list on the Internet and I recalled her daughters' names. Sadly, I found her on a GoFundMe account her daughter started last year. It turns out she has some very serious cancer. Her phone number was listed, and I reached out to her. She was happy to hear from me and we will talk soon when she has a good day. Her energy is up and down so it all depends. It makes me very sad as she is only 68 and such a giving and amazing lady.

Since January, I've been working diligently to create a life that will support me going back to my writing career. I took the bull by the horns and stripped our budget down from over $3,100 a month to $2,482. The Internet is gone and the extra phone is gone. We tried an antenna but got no channels in this area, so I exchanged it for a $30 DVD player. We have been ordering movies from the library and found some good movies at Goodwill. The boys play like crazy now and I only wish I had done this sooner. We all gather and watch the best movies every night, but during the day, we play and do chores and schoolwork.

My cheap laptop died, and it made me stop and look at this as a sign, especially since the laptop was less than five months old. It wasn't like I was taking it into the shower to work or the boys were making mud pies on the thing. It was gently used since the laptop before it died in under a year.

So, it died from nothing other than cheapness, and I sat in my yard and felt bummed and a little lost. I had a long talk with my boys' godmother about the spiritual world and being in the moment. I sat on a wooden bench that was made for me by two men that I gave the black walnut wood to when we had the tree taken down in our front yard. I watched my chubby little dog, Molly roll about on the ground with glee. I listened to Arjan and Sam laughing and playing with nothing more than a small bottle of bubbles I bought Sam at the hospice thrift store for $0.50.

I returned to the moment. It felt like balm.

We are our only enemy. We are our own slave makers. We are the only ones that have this illusion that we must do this or that or that we can't do this or that. It reminds me of the photo of the big, strong horse tied to a light, plastic chair and thinking it couldn't move. We are the creators of our prisons.

I didn't make any decisions about the laptop for days. I thought about the message that I was being given.

After a short time, my husband and his boss chose a new laptop for me that included a four-year warranty, as it is obvious I need one of those. When the laptop arrived, I took it to the library to register it using their Internet. The library was closed due to COVID-19. Another sign? I registered the laptop from my car in their parking lot.

I came home and asked Spirit for guidance. I needed a clear sign as to what to do about my career path. The next morning, I set up the laptop to download my videos so I could edit them in Movie Maker. For some reason, on this new laptop, I can't download videos or photos without the Internet. It was suddenly very clear. It was becoming too complicated. I was going upstream. I decided right then and there to be done. I deleted all the videos and photos and let it all go. I had great videos, that's what my ego told me. I deleted them anyway. We will try to rationalize or talk ourselves into not quitting something. But when it's time, the best thing to do is just cut the cord and turn to the light and say, "What next?!"

When you ask, the Universe answers, but you need to pay attention and be ready and courageous enough to act right now. The signs are often a few subtle moments, but if you tune in, you know what they are telling you to do.

Chapter 4

Be Broke for the Time Being and Focus on Creating

I am now focused on two things: raising my boys and my writing. I have found that since finally whittling it down to two priorities and eliminating the other three or four jobs, my energy is abundant, and my mood is playful and focused. I'm no longer spread thin and feeling tired upon waking and looking about at all I must do.

That used to happen. I would wake up, go to the kitchen and see the sink full of dishes from the night before because, let's be honest, we sometimes don't have the energy at the end of the night to wash that last sinkful that always seems to grow right before bedtime. I would look about at hairballs on the floor and toys left out and I knew that I had a long day ahead of cleaning and cooking, filming, editing, writing, researching...and I would feel my energy drain right then.

A strong cup of coffee and some music sometimes helped but then I would get on YouTube to find a cleaning video to help inspire me and before I knew it, time was flying away as I got lost in videos or constantly checked the Internet between a chore or two. I would check my email, even though it's usually garbage. I would check my book stats which only needed to be checked once a week if at all, but I would check a few times a day. I would check YouTube repeatedly to reply to comments, and when I had my blog and Patreon, I did the same thing with them. I wasted hours on comments and then got lost on other channels. I didn't realize how many hours a day I kept myself distracted from real work until I got rid of it all.

Not everyone is like this and not everyone has to get rid of the Internet to focus. I'm just one of those special people. I'm like a child that will find many other things to get into to avoid my work. I've always been like this. I remember cleaning the house as a girl and I'd be tidying up the magazines and would stop to look through them for long periods of time, forgetting about the work ahead of me.

Now I wake up and the house is tidy because every night before bed, I insist that the toys are picked up. I also wash the last of the dishes and give the kitchen a quick wipedown. I set up the percolator on the stove with water and coffee grounds. There is something about waking up to a tidy house and a clean kitchen that gives one the best start to a productive day.

I brew coffee and spend time with my family, the boys make the beds, I cook breakfast, or we have a simple meal of toast. I make big batches of homemade wheat bread that I make very healthy by adding a lot of wheat germ and wheat bran. I add wheat germ and wheat bran to everything since I read *JADAM Organic Farming: The Way to Ultra-Low-Cost Agriculture.* Youngsang Cho writes about the health of our bodies and the health of our soil, and he encourages us to eat whole foods and not peel the fruits or vegetables (although I can't see myself eating the orange rind anytime soon), and to eat brown rice and whole grains. I immediately switched back to brown rice and I make my tortillas, bread, and pizza dough with wheat, bran, and wheat germ. I buy all these ingredients very inexpensively in the bulk section at WinCo.

For me to focus on writing and give up making all other sources of income, I had to reduce the income. To do it on paper is the easy part, to live it requires some work and a lot of NOT doing. Not shopping, not browsing thrift stores, not getting online to browse, and not watching commercials or advertisements to tempt us. It helps to have no Internet and only watch movies on DVDs. You are no longer subject to anything that might lead you astray.

Next, we take inventory of what we have. I made sure that I had all the bedding and kitchen tools, and I ordered the last of my trees - two chestnuts and a pluot to pollinate the beautiful pluot plum I have near the porch. I just went through the basket of garden seeds today, and I'm thrilled to see that I have almost all the seeds I'll need for this spring and summer. I only need a few more packets. That totals up to less than $10 for a seasonful of organic produce. We still have the winter garden going and it's doing well. We even planted potatoes and another batch of mustard greens so we will see. I harvested the first of my mustard greens the other day and we had them with brown rice and chicken.

We planted a small orchard when we moved up here. We moved to this house in 2020 and just as we moved our last truckload up the mountain, the whole world shut down for a quarantine that would last over a year. When the government announced a shutdown, I ran off to a large nursery and filled trolleys with fruit trees and berry bushes. We planted nuts, fruits, berries and then we fenced off an 800 square foot area and tilled it up. We didn't have much success with the first few plantings. The first garden was in straight clay soil and too late. Then we hauled in two truckloads of horse manure we got for free at a horse ranch and started a compost pile but it's just us four and we can only make so much compost. We add kitchen scraps, grass trimmings, and leaves from the huge English walnut trees that hang over our yard. Unfortunately, the winter garden was planted too late because I thought of it too late and didn't know what I was doing. Then summer comes again, and we are in a drought and dealing with fires in the area, so we stop watering, and the smoke blocks the sun.

This winter we raked up all the leaves and piled them in the garden along with our compost piles for easier access and mixing. We now have a garden book from local master gardeners and it's all about growing, what to grow, and how to grow in this area. Not only that, we have a handy dandy planting guide as well. We kept amending the soil and tilling it in to mix with the clay and finally, we had some success with the winter garden despite the crazy snow.

We have killed trees, planted in the wrong season altogether, and made a lot of mistakes. However, as painful as mistakes are (and sometimes expensive), you learn a lot. This year we know how to work the soil, that the no-dig method doesn't work in our plot, when to plant, when to start seeds, and how to deal with leaf curl, fungus, and aphids. We also know how to mulch properly, how much to water, and so much more.

This year I am hoping for great abundance, and more than that, I want to enjoy the process. You need to have fun with it and then gardening becomes a very joyful and therapeutic craft. You can grow so much organic food and save a lot of money year-round if you have a decent zone and learn to can and dehydrate. Even if your zone is not so gardening friendly and summers are short, and/or the soil is poor, you can still do it. Look at Alaska homesteaders and other channels with short seasons. There is a video on YouTube I love so much: *My Urban Garden* on the NFB channel. It inspires me greatly. It is about a woman in Nova Scotia who gardens in a tiny yard. The soil is terrible, and her summers are short and not that warm, yet she grows seven months out of the year and produces a lot of food for her family of five. I highly suggest watching it for motivation. It's a charming older video as well.

Thanks to a woman cleaning out her garage and deciding that canning was not in her future, I have a lot of preserving equipment now, but I did start with a water bath pot and some tools from Walmart. I found my first batch of canning jars on Craigslist for cheap. The woman was moving and had boxes of unopened jars. I think it's a little harder to find deals because so many people are now into gardening and canning again.

I learned to make triple berry jam and spaghetti sauce using a water bath canning method. I also learned to freeze corn by cutting the kernels off the cob and putting them in a sugar water solution. I even made dilly beans! I haven't canned in a couple of years, but this year is my lucky year.

I think of gardening as growing your own produce aisle. I go to the health food store and see the cost of nuts and fruits we love, and after gasping and clutching my chest, I go to a local nursery and buy the trees and bushes and vines and have my husband plant them in our yard. It may take a few years as some trees take up to five to seven years to produce, but one day we will not have to pay $13 for a pound of chestnuts or $4 for a pound of nectarines. We use a lot of garlic and onions, and last year we had fantastic luck with garlic. Fresh food that is picked and cooked up within minutes is so flavorful and loaded with vitamins. We only plant what we eat.

Gardening requires water, but you can save a lot by using a lot of mulch and water from your tub. You can also use water from your kiddy pool, washing machine, and even dish water if you use specific detergents and soaps. You can Google which laundry and dish soap is harmless for gardens. My husband is planning to do a drip system this year. Last year we had an above-ground pool and when it got dirty, we bought a pool pump, attached the hose, and watered every tree and the garden with the water, not wasting a drop. I use the tub water for my porch plants and house plants even in the winter. Our water usage keeps going down each year, even in the summer, despite having so many trees and a large garden.

Besides learning to garden to ensure fresh, affordable groceries in the future, I have a long list of things in the house to help save a lot of money.

Take our reusable stuff, for example. We have a Berkey water filter, a Bona cloth mop, a steam mop, and we use all cloth napkins and kitchen towels, and real plates and utensils, even when we have dinner parties and gatherings (not that we've had any of those in the last two years). I save old, worn shirts and towels for cleaning rags and in place of paper towels. I even have cloth feminine pads and reusable straws.

I watch some of the budget grocery trips on YouTube and I wondered what one would save by NOT buying paper plates, napkins, Swiffer wet mop pads, paper towels, bottled water, juice, and all the snacks. I know since stopping all buying of treats, convenience foods, and frozen foods, our grocery bill dropped by hundreds in a month.

Here's the breakdown for the math people, I did this just for you.

Everything is from Walmart and I'm listing the cheapest brands or generic brands. Not everyone has a WinCo, but Walmart is everywhere.

A 12-pack of paper towels costs $20.98. Say you use one and a half rolls a week. A one year supply would cost approximately $135.

Water. We go through three gallons per day (we don't drink milk, soda, or juice). Not only do we drink it, but we use it for cooking as well. Three gallons (each gallon is $1.12) a day for a year = $1,226.

Swiffer Sweeper Wet Mopping Pads: one box a month at $23.59 would be $283.08 a year.

Napkins, 150 count: one pack a month at $3.75 comes out to $45 per year.

Paper plates, 150 count: one pack per month at $10.48 would be $125.76 a year.

Feminine pads at $3.82 for a year is $45.84.

This is a total of over $1860 you lose annually. We save this much.

Also, if you have babies, diapers are $39.94 a month per baby. That's $479.28 a year. Add that to the pile.

And we haven't even touched on groceries!

I am deep, deep into scratch cooking right now. I've been getting into it for years but here I am, a decade of homemaking later and I am finally going all the way with it.

I recently acquired some used copies of the *Make-A-Mix* cookbook series by Karine Eliason. I am very much in love here. I have already made the granola batch two or three times, a big batch of cracker mix, and sweet bread mix because we love the Date and Nut Loaf recipe at tea time.

I enjoy thumbing through these books and highlighting my favorites for the future. If you could only have three cookbooks for your life, *Make-A-Mix Cookery and More Make-A-Mix Cookery*, along with the more modern *Make-A-Mix* (confusing because they didn't change the title, but it has new recipes) would have everything you could ever want or need.

Of course, I did add to my small cookbook library with a few more books. First was *More Make Your Own Groceries* (the first edition was priced at $89 so that was out), and then I added *Make Your Own Convenience Foods* by Donald and Joan German, and *Better Than Store-Bought* by Helen Witty and Elizabeth Schneider Colchie. These are old books but get rave reviews and with this library, I can make everything I would normally buy at the store. Skip the chemicals and colors, the extra fat and sugar, save tons of money, and gain pride in stocking your pantry with your kitchen skills.

It is far easier than it seems. I now make big batches of cracker or pancake mixes that store from three to six months and make many, many servings. I used to buy the big 5 lb. box of Krusteaz pancake mix. Now I can make a big batch of healthier pancake mix for less.

If you buy store bread, mixes, premade foods, both frozen and boxed, junk foods, cakes, cookies, and the like, your grocery bill will be triple what it costs to just keep it simple with a 50 lb. bag of flour, some yeast, produce, oil, and meat. If you can do without the meat and dairy, you are in for an even smaller grocery bill.

I did a search online for 25 lb. of flour and I found Bob's Red Mill All-Purpose Flour for $20.99 and then I found Kroger All-Purpose Flour for $6.99 per 25 lb. bag - amazing! Whole wheat flour at 25 lb. is also much cheaper. You can even get organic for $17.82 through Azure Standard.

With a 25 lb. bag of white flour and a 25 lb. bag of wheat flour, you can make several loaves of bread, your pancake mix, cracker mix, cake mixes, cookie mixes, pasta, tortillas...all the things you buy packaged. And these mixes will be cleaner and healthier.

There are 90 cups of flour in a 25 lb. bag. I use about 5 cups to make two loaves of bread. That is 18 loaves of bread. If I buy the flour at $20.99 that is $1.16 per loaf, but you need to throw in a few more cents for yeast. Now, I did find some cheap white bread at Walmart for $0.89 but the homemade version will be a lot healthier. If you use Kroger's flour at $6.99, then it is $0.38 a loaf.

I can't do the math on everything, but some packaged things *are* cheaper. For instance, macaroni and cheese costs $0.48 per box at WinCo. That price is less expensive than making it from scratch. You can Google anything and do the math.

When I was working all the time filming, writing, homeschooling, and a list of other odds and ends to keep the home running full speed, I would often buy store-bought bread and we liked the good stuff at over $4.99 per loaf. I would buy frozen pierogies, vegetable dumplings, and frozen pizzas. Some frozen pizzas are dirt cheap, but they are skimpy and little. Nothing beats a loaded homemade pan pizza that is thick and filling. Now and then, I would buy a Stouffer's lasagna along with bagged specialty salads at $3.99 for a small bag. For $10 I can make a huge bin of organic salad for four people that will serve us large helpings for at least four meals.

When I buy frozen and packaged foods my grocery bill is over $350 for a couple of weeks, maybe more; especially if you throw in snacks and tortillas.

In my opinion, the cheapest grocery bill would consist of this: wheat flour, white flour, yeast, oil, onions, garlic, potatoes, green cabbage, carrots, apples, bananas, oranges if in season, pinto beans, and brown rice. I believe this is the healthiest, most nutritious, and cheapest way to eat. You then add a few whole chickens, some ground beef, a block of cheese, some eggs, coffee, milk for the coffee, and you're a happy person.

Now, this sounds like a dull monthly grocery list but if you have a well-stocked pantry with seasonings and some extras you can make up so many hearty dishes: casseroles and fried potatoes, loaded burritos, lasagna, delicious spaghetti, soups, pot roast, enchiladas...

As we master a garden, we will be less dependent on grocery store produce. My pantry is well stocked. I have all sorts of herbs and spices, masalas, chili seasoning, onion soup mix, Worcestershire sauce, mustards, creamed corn, pasta, polenta, rolled oats, lentils, 13 bean mix, black beans, pinto beans, brown rice, white rice, lots of wheat (maybe too much), and white all-purpose flour. I have cornbread mix (but I'll be making my own soon), cream of mushroom soup, mushroom gravy, cranberry jelly, potato flakes, milk powder, and powdered egg substitutes. You can also stock up on ghee for butter because it's shelf-stable. I also have plenty of yeast, baking powder, baking soda, wheat bran, and wheat germ.

I stock up when the money is available. Recently we had a huge shopping trip to WinCo, and I stocked my pantry very well for $652. It filled shelves and the chest freezer. That was last month, and I'm still working from this pantry stock and won't have to buy any seasonings, herbs, wheat, beans, or rice for months.

I watched a news clip called *The Most Frugal Moms In The Country*, on a YouTube channel called TrishSchmiderz. It's about two mothers who worked for the same company and were laid off. They both practiced frugality in different ways. One hired an insurance broker to make sure she got the best prices on her medications and such, used coupons and compared prices at various stores, cut her hair between salon visits, and portioned out the meat. She said the best time to tighten up was when the economy was good. That is so true. When you have the money flowing in is the best time to save and prepare. Not to say you don't have fun as well, but you can have fun on a budget.

The other woman was a single parent and she had done so well with saving money that she was able to take three years off to be with her kids after getting laid off. She paid her house off in five years. She bought her furniture at thrift stores and bought a used car in cash.

I have had years where I didn't spend money and worked with a grocery envelope. I've had years of spending money and being a frequent shopper on Amazon. Fortunately, most of what I bought on Amazon and elsewhere was for the house, garden, yard, kids, and pets; not that frivolous. I also had those years in my youth where I blew through thousands of dollars and had nothing to show for it, and there is nothing more disappointing than that.

Chapter 5

How I Prepared to Work Less

I've mentioned a few books that had such a big impact on me that I began a life transformation after reading them. Lately, I have been rereading those books in order to become even stronger and clearer about my direction.

As I've mentioned previously, the first book was *Essentialism* by Greg McKeown. The second was *What Falls From The Sky* by Esther Emery, and the last book might seem strange, sort of like, "Which one of these is not like the other?" but it made a big impact as well. That book is *Evicted: Poverty And Profit In The American City*, by Matthew Desmond.

I read *Essentialism* when I had a hundred plates spinning and was adding more all the time. I was fried and bitchy, to say the least, and was not doing well in any area, just keeping things going. My work lacked fun and enthusiasm, my parenting skills sucked, my house was surface cleaned, and I felt tired and irritable all the time. I did weird stuff like "retire" from my channel, which was smart at the time since I had added fostering to the pot, and I did have to focus on that and my kids. But then I deleted my channel when we were being harassed. If you are in the public eye there are always the hecklers. But I was so tired and worn that I couldn't take it. Then I started another channel and blog right away. Was it out of habit or addiction to being noticed? Was it an obligation? Maybe all of it, but what I should have done was just take some time and space to find what was most important and, at the time, running my home and tending to children was where my focus needed to be.

I began thinking about a time when I was happy and calm in my life and realized it was back when the boys were tiny, and I was completely focused on them along with my housework. I cooked and cleaned, nursed, read to the boys, sat with them while they rolled and crawled and waddled about discovering things. I wasn't online at all; I did have Facebook back then, but I hated it from the start, so I just stayed off it. I wasn't interested in YouTube as it wasn't that great back then. Not like now, with a million channels on everything you can think up. We had an antenna and got 13 channels. TCM was for old classic movies, a channel with old westerns, and PBS with wonderful cartoons. I would watch some TV in the evenings, but mostly played the radio, Disney songs, or nursery songs for the boys. I read to them, and I read clean, delightful novels for myself. That was life. Very slow, quiet, and peaceful. Not a lot of outside noise. We lived far from a big town and planned our grocery shopping on Sundays. I had an old school friend who would visit once a week, and an old neighbor named Alice who would sit with me under the big magnolias in the front and chat sometimes. I didn't watch the news, didn't get on social media, and I didn't use our Internet.

I was very pleasant and sweet back then. I had no worries, and all that restlessness left me. I surrendered to slow life in the country and took up reading to entertain myself.

But we moved after a couple of years and slowly, life got busier. I made it that way. It started innocently. I started writing and learned how to publish for free on KDP Amazon. Then we moved into our first house which was a real fixer-upper and I was so into homesteading in town. I discovered some good channels on YouTube and wanted to share my delightful life. Ah, but then I learned about monetizing the channel and the green-eyed monster of greed and comparison came into my life. I wanted the channel to grow, grow, grow. I wanted more subscribers and more money, and I compared myself to others and became disheartened and dissatisfied. I judged myself and my work instead of just having fun.

I regret those years. I was so occupied with producing that I often feel I wasn't present in my life. I was in my head and thinking about business and money instead of focusing on family and home.

When we moved up to this mountain town, I was very happy, but I worked myself into the ground with everything. Along came that book. I lay in bed at night and my mind reminded me of the quiet times out in the country so long ago.

It took a good year to get to this destination. I planned and pondered, but guilt, obligation, money worries, and fear of losing all I had worked for weighed heavily on me. I had to overcome this. It is what McKeown talks about in the book: "Sunk Cost Trap."

This is a big one to look at. It's when we invest so much time and energy or money into something but it's a flop or failure *or* it's not giving us what we had hoped for, yet we keep at it, keep working, keep throwing money at it because, well, we already invested so much, we might as well keep going.

My channel had a lot of good and positive and we had a great community, so it was not a waste or a flop. But when I thought about letting it go and returning my focus to writing, I struggled with the decision to let it go since it had been my way of life for years.

Over the year, I slowly began removing things. It all made money, but quite frankly, small amounts for the hours I put in. The blog made $100 every six months and being that I wrote almost daily, that worked out to a few cents per hour.

I began preparing for leaner times. I knew that if I were to go back to writing full-time, it would take time to refocus and study. YouTube was a good source of income. During the holidays I made a whopping $2,000 in November, but most months I made an average of $575. That's grocery money, and during the holidays, it's an opportunity to bring in the big bucks to save or pay off small debts.

But then I calculated the hours I spent making videos, editing (I use the term loosely as I wasn't the best, but I did some work), researching, thinking about the videos, uploading, getting back to comments, and working on improving. I realized that if I put in, say, 4 hours a day, every day, and made an average of $575 and sometimes less each month, I'm making about $4.79 an hour.

What if I focused on writing, and *only* writing and built a good career that one day brought in more money? What if I did it from the heart and loved every day of it?

The other part of choosing writing over a channel is privacy. I no longer film our life nor must I find the space to film my chatty videos. No longer do I let everyone into my life. My community was lovely, and I was fortunate, but there are other parts of the public who make things unpleasant and disturbing. I now have some privacy back and my family's life returned to normal.

The biggest sign for me was when my boys asked that I not film them anymore. I was never that into it with how weird things get online. But they are always here and if I'm to film naturally, they get into the film now and then.

The relief and joy I felt after making the decision confirmed that I was on the right path. The energy I have once again for my writing, my family, and housework is abundant. It feels good to begin a new journey. I am fully inspired to study and write every day and now my mind is no longer busy. I feel renewed.

None of this change has been hard. It's been easier, better, and more fun than I envisioned. I don't miss my home phone at all like I thought I would. I have earbuds and I place my cell phone in my apron pocket and chat with girlfriends while doing chores. I couldn't do that with the home phone. It had no earphone plug and I had to sit and hold the big receiver as I would chat. Sometimes I felt agitated as I looked at the pile of dishes or the porch that needed a good sweeping. Now I can socialize *and* get projects done!

How To Prepare For Lean Years While You Learn Your New Craft

In this whole year of pondering and mustering up the courage to leap back into a full-time writing life, I knew I wouldn't make more money right away. I have several books out on Amazon already. I've been writing for about seven years. I have produced a lot of nonfiction about my homemaking life and about five fictional books. Fiction is not easy. You need to get into that mood and work hard for a long time before you start to write some decent stories. I have only written one fictional book in five years and because all I talk about, think about, and write about is homemaking and frugality, well, my fiction was worse than ever. All the characters would wind up on budgets and had to grow gardens to feed themselves. My stories would turn into stories of canning and getting by. That doesn't sell books in the fiction world. But it's all I know right now; it's all my mind chews on daily.

I will need time to expel the old life and fill up on creative fictional books and movies. I will be making time daily to write *and* study the craft. Some say you don't need to but that brings me to another part of Greg McKeown's book in *Essentialism*.

Back in the early 1900s, two explorers, Robert Falcon Scott and Roald Amundsen, wanted to be the first to reach the South Pole. Both had the same goal - to be the first to reach the South Pole and be the first team in history to do so.

Mr. Amundsen studied and read voraciously. He prepared for anything and everything that could go wrong. He packed 3 tons of food for his team, and he had stored food and supplies along the path for the return home, marking them with several markers miles apart so they couldn't be missed. He overpacked and was over-prepared. On the trip, he had his team pace themselves to do so many miles a day, but not overdo it. They rested plenty. Slow and steady wins the race and it's not just a children's fable. They made it to the South Pole and back without much trouble.

Mr. Scott didn't read or study, he hoped for the best-case scenario in all things. He only packed the bare minimum.

He only packed one ton of food for the team. He had stored supplies for the return but only marked it with one marker and if they were off course by even a smidge, they would miss it. He pushed and drove his team to exhaustion on clear days to make up for blizzard days when they couldn't get far or move at all. His team suffered frostbite, exhaustion, and hunger. They all died on the trip. Very morbid, I know.

What does this teach us? Prepare, and over-prepare in all things. It certainly doesn't hurt to do so.

Despite making royalties on pre-published books, I can never count on how much will come in monthly. It could be a thousand dollars one month and less than three hundred the next. I have let go of at least three other income sources over the last year.

I refuse to get another side job or hustle ever again. My jobs are tending to my family and homesteading.

I prepare for us to live on one income, and when extra money flows in we save it or pay a bill. To prepare for anything and everything, we prepare to not make any royalties or extra money. Whether this happens or not, we have one income for sure and we get rid of everything that isn't a basic need such as shelter, water, gas, solar, garbage, groceries, some insurance, and phone. We then reduce even those bills if we can.

We stock up, and overstock in case we don't have funds later. We save money while we can.

Early last spring there was a 50% off sale at Savers. The store is an hour and a half away from us, but this location is huge, clean, and organized. All the rich city folk drop off their stuff, so I know there is a treasure of things there. We took a cash envelope and headed there. I stocked up on two to three years of very nice clothes for the boys. Everything: pajamas, play clothes, school clothes, clothes for all seasons, jackets for all seasons, warm hats, backpacks, and scarves. I stocked up on clothes for both Bali and I, linens, a quilt, books, toys, and games. I will only have to buy underwear and shoes over the next few years. I've already stocked up on socks and snow boots that will last a couple of years.

With the extra money, I bought sturdy thermoses and travel containers for the boys' school lunches along with stainless steel water bottles. These things will last.

We had a small Berkey, but I bought a 3-gallon Berkey and am glad I did as it saves us thousands a year. It cost $450 but pays for itself in less than 6 months and since you only buy the filters every six years, you can save close to $12,000 in that period.

I stocked up on more bedding when it snowed heavily over here. We have Presto Heat Dish heaters that save on electricity and gas and keep us warm. My gas bill has decreased greatly since we just turn them on every now and then to take the chill off, moving it from room to room, depending on where we are hanging out in the house.

I also stocked up on candles and scents. Those are more luxurious items, but they make the home cozy.

I bought books for my home library such as the *Make-A-Mix* books along with some gardening books.

I also stocked the pantry with plenty of dried goods and bulk seasonings. I stocked up on 10 lb. of baking soda, four gallons of vinegar, and gallons of Dawn dish soap for making all my cleaners. Every time I shopped, I picked up laundry detergent and Zote soap bars (the best thing ever for getting stains out).

We are fully stocked with shampoo, conditioner, soap, toothpaste, hair dye, lotions, razors, and wax.

We splurged on a 7 cu ft deep freezer and filled it up. With Bali's help, I created a pantry in the laundry room as it's cool and dry in there. I only use the dryer in the winter and it's airy enough to not create moisture.

I stocked up on coffee, of course.

Now, all this won't last us years. But it gives us a good start and as I find sales and figure out coupons, I can keep things well-stocked.

I've been reading about gardening like crazy and a master gardener moved in next door. What luck!

We installed solar and a whole house generator and what a smart move because this winter's storms knocked out so many power lines, we didn't have power for five days. PG&E will only get more expensive over here.

We've been planting fruit and nut trees and amending the soil for a couple of years now. This is a good investment.

We will be switching to Mint Mobile service for the cell phones and that'll save us $45 each month.

We have old vehicles but take good care of them and I drive mine as little as possible to save on gas and wear and tear. We live right in town so we can either walk everywhere or take a local bus that stops across the street from us. This is great to have if the cars break down. My husband commutes but if he had to, he has a job right here in town anytime he wants and could bike, walk or take the bus. We could get along fine without cars. No repairs, oil changes, registration fees, insurance, gas...oh, what a dream. That might come next.

We try to do all we can by hand. Bali has repaired things on the car and truck, installed sinks, built greenhouses, and much more. I cook almost everything from scratch to save money now, and do all the housecleaning, gardening, finances, and homeschooling. I don't prepare our income taxes for good reason. Last time I did them we owed. I know my limits and math is one of them.

I've begun rereading the books that inspired me along with *The Complete Tightwad Gazette* to glean more tricks and get me in that mindset.

Another cookbook I forgot to mention is *Good and Cheap* by Leanne Brown. It is a cookbook created for people on a limited food stamp budget, but of course, anyone can benefit from it. If you go on her website, you can download the PDF for free. This book has everything, including recipes for pierogies and dumplings so I don't need to buy those anymore.

Chapter 6

Movies That Have Inspired Change

We have a Roku TV, and it is wonderful. But with no Internet, there is no Roku. As I mentioned previously, we tried an antenna but got no reception, not even with it placed on the roof. So we exchanged it for a DVD player, and we have been in movie heaven ever since.

When the money was flowing, I invested in a larger TV. Not obscenely large, but large enough to enjoy movies. We love movies. The brand was generic, so it was cheap at $273. I don't regret it. Now, with movies at night, we are in heaven. It saves us almost $50 plus in not going to the theater.

I love movies that inspire or get me to think about things. We watched *Spirited Away* recently. It's about greed and gluttony in all forms; how greed will devour us, and gluttony will transform us into something unattractive. A little girl and her parents are on their way to a new town and wind up on a side road. They come upon a tunnel that they decide to explore and discover a strange, abandoned town. The parents find a buffet of hot foods and gorge themselves until they turn into large pigs. A spirit helps the girl. To survive, she gets a job working in a bathhouse for spirits. There, a spirit named No Face is let in and tempts the workers with shiny gold that isn't real, but they don't know that. They jump over hoops to give him whatever he wants for more of the shiny gold. He devours everything and is never satisfied; he even begins to eat them one by one.

I won't share the end, but this was another sign and push to get off the treadmill. So many of us work, work, work, always wanting more and more and more. We grab at the shiny baubles of fake gold, eat too much, drink too much, and live in poor health mentally, physically, and spiritually. Look at our society. Most people work over 60 hours a week. Most people are now overweight. Being chubby is now normal. When I was a kid, the chubby person was the oddity, now a thin person is hard to find. People have main jobs and side hustles. I see it with YouTube channels. The bigger channels have Facebook, blogs, and Instagram. They link products and sell things on the side. They may have families and I wonder how they have time for them with all the work. I am speaking from experience here.

Everyone is on their phones. People carry their phones in their hands, they don't put them away in their bags or purses. They take them everywhere, to the toilet, to the restaurant...like an infant.

I watched another, more modern movie called *Jexi*. It is about a man who learned to live on his phone from childhood. His parents kept handing him the phone to keep him busy. He can't even find his way home without his phone. He is so socially awkward that when he gets a chance to make friends or date a girl, he lies about fake social calendars. He lives on his phone, rarely looking up to glance at his surroundings. One day it's smashed, and he goes into a cell phone store to get a new one and the sales lady goes off on him. She says she sees guys like him all the time, they are worse than crackheads. She says, "A crackhead will at least leave the house occasionally to look for more crack. A crackhead will talk to other crackheads."

This obsession with our phones and social media and being face planted to a screen, setting up bells to let us know of every call, email, and Facebook post so we don't miss out is not normal. Yet, when I share that we don't have Internet, most are either interested or like that idea, but some people seem perplexed. "How do the boys do homeschool?" Paper books; they are still around. "How long can you keep this up?" I'm not doing the absurd.

The Industrial Period began in 1760 and has been growing exponentially over the past 260 years. The computer age is maybe 70 years old, and this period with social media is said to have started in the '70s but didn't truly begin until the '90s. However, it was not too appealing until around 2003 with the development of sites such as Friendster, MySpace, Facebook, Twitter, Snapchat, Instagram and YouTube, to name a few. So, in our 2,000,000 years of humanity, we have only had this experience of social media and phone obsession for a little over sixteen years.

Unfortunately, mental health issues have increased. People are suffering more than ever from depression, isolation, lack of sleep, stress and worry, and feelings of inadequacy. Teenagers are being greatly affected and teen and tween suicides are a big problem in our communities. Poor mental health and suicides are being strongly linked to social media by hundreds of studies. All you have to do is Google the topic and see the sad results. There is a documentary on Netflix, *The Social Dilemma*, all about this topic and I would strongly suggest seeing it and doing your research before letting your teenagers live on their phones and have social media accounts.

We are not used to all this bombardment of ideas, information, opinions, and all the bullying and hate that is included in living online. It is a whole new world, and our minds aren't prepared for it. We are not able to adjust to it. It may seem so fun at first, but we don't fare well in the end. A little is fine, but most people spend an average of almost 7 hours a day on the Internet. We are spending a quarter of our lives online. If we spend 7 hours of our day on the Internet and we sleep for 7 or 8 hours (most people don't anymore), that leaves 10 hours, and those are for work and commuting. Where is the family time? And time for hobbies and building dreams?

It is true; we are a society of phone addicts, social media addicts, and addicts of every kind. According to Indian yoga guru, Sadhguru, 70% of the population is addicted to something: food, pills of all kinds - for pain, to sleep, keep calm, or be somewhat happy. Interestingly, there are warnings on the "happy" pills that say they may cause suicidal thoughts. I'm thinking that a pill that may cause you to kill yourself is not working very well as a mood elevator. People get high to connect to Source and get cracked out to get stuff done but most meth addicts only move piles around. People drink themselves silly on the weekends because "we deserve to get smashed."

To be quiet and present is hard now. It's not complicated enough. Let's get a stack of self-help books and study how to be happy.

Or why don't we just unplug for a bit and see how that affects our moods and lives? And don't just unplug for a few days. Give it a couple of weeks or a whole month.

I was excited to start this experiment but as the days drew closer to the new year, I found I was a little fearful and nervous about it. Then a cosmic thing occurred: it snowed so much one night, and the snow was so wet and heavy following torrential rain and windstorms that power went out in our county and many surrounding counties. For days and weeks. We were lucky, being in town, we had power in five days but being that I'm not always the sharpest tool in the shed, I didn't realize that the Internet worked when I ran the generator, so we thought the unplugging had begun early. We spent five days playing in the snow listening to the radio and reading books again. By the first of the new year, we adjusted to not having Internet. After the first real week, I knew this was a good life. We had gone back to the old days.

Chapter 7

Making a Home Sanctuary and Zen-like Living

Ok, so let's review the last two books. Thought I forgot? I do drift off on many paths, but I will get back to the point eventually. I also want to talk about the documentary *How To Cook Your Life*.

What Falls From The Sky is a good book. Esther Emery wrote it after her one-year experience completely offline. No Internet, I don't think she even did TV. Brutal. She didn't use the ATM or Google Maps. It was cash and paper maps. I just reordered the book but what stuck with me was when she said, "In that year I found my soul."

She healed her marriage, herself, found her love of God, love of baking and nesting, and learned to slow way, way down. After that, her family moved up to the mountains and started an off-grid life. She had two YouTube channels going and her kids even started a channel. Then they must have realized they were getting right back into that online life again and not being present, because some years ago they posted a vlog about a lazy summer and then disappeared. I'm only assuming, but I feel like I never want to return to the Internet in our home. My kids howl when I say this so I don't speak these words out loud, but I feel like if I brought it all back, I would cry deeply.

Yes, there are times when it's strangely quiet and times when I sit and feel old, musty feelings that I previously kept busy enough to ignore. I go through blues, but they only last a few hours. It's old stuff I had no time for, and it has to come up and be released.

Mostly, I hear my kids talking and laughing, like right now as I type. They are on the porch giggling and making up stories and jokes. They think they're comedians. I have the radio playing some old '90s hit and I'm in my bedroom typing away.

There were items on my to-do list that I thought would be real issues, like taxes. This year I had so much paperwork to send to my tax lady and I have no printer/scanner or fax machine without Internet. The libraries are closed again. But it turned out to be the easiest year of filing ever. Thanks to modern technology, I just sent pictures of all the paperwork through my phone. I was done within minutes.

Everything I thought would be complicated has been simple.

Time slows down and I'm no longer bombarded with information. I'm not wasting time sitting in front of a laptop watching others doing whatever. I have quiet. I don't know that I've found my soul just yet. I still have data on my phone. That is, until next month when we switch phone plans. I have chosen to have very little data just for the essentials, and then I will find all my souls, present and past.

Now we come to the third book, *Evicted: Poverty And Profit In An American City*. Matthew Desmond writes this book from an emotionally detached way. He gets to know the people he is writing about, both tenants facing eviction as well as the slumlords. He writes about various people. A drug addict, an older woman with a spending problem, a single mother who has gone through some rough times and continues to have rough times, a single, handicapped father, and a couple of families. He gets to know a couple who proudly own several slum units as well as the managers of a slummy trailer park. He simply tells their stories as he observes the unfolding of troubles and evictions, some that happen over and over.

I was leery about reading something that I thought would be written dramatically and would wear on each nerve with the hardships and suffering. Instead, he wrote the book in such a way that you can observe with him and make up your own opinions of what is going on. He discusses the history of slums and poverty over hundreds of years, and in the end, he explores several solutions to this ever-worsening problem. There are a couple of happy endings, and he discusses the importance of home for the human spirit and family and community.

I won't go into my feelings about all this, but I highly recommend this book for a few reasons. One reason is understanding and fostering compassion. Whether people get into bad situations because of drugs, poor choices, mental illness, or plain foolishness, I believe that if we can understand it a bit, we can be more compassionate. We can understand sometimes people are taken advantage of in ways that keep them in the cycle of defeat. It's hard to climb out of a deep pit of hardship that has been built over years of wrong turns and disadvantages.

The other reason for reading this book is to find a whole new appreciation for having shelter, especially affordable shelter. It is advised to pay no more than 30% of your income to rent or mortgage. However, in this market, most are paying over 50% of their incomes on rent and struggling to cover expenses. Some people on government assistance that don't have help with housing are paying 70% or more and that makes covering regular bills very hard. It's hard to pay bills and keep up with the rent if it's overpriced.

We pay anywhere from 40% to over 50% for our mortgage depending on if there is extra money coming in per month. Fortunately, we have no loans, credit cards, car payments, or debt. We recently went a little crazy with home improvements and had quite the tab at The Home Depot, then the dog needed a tooth pulled, the car broke down, and the laptop I work from died. All of a sudden we had bills, bills, bills. I was still working on YouTube, so I had some great royalties come in from my channel and we were able to pay off most things. But what happens when you don't have extra work and cash coming in? What happens if you have no savings? And what do you do to build a savings if 70% of your income is just for rent or mortgage? This is a scary place to be. And so many people are just getting the bills paid with a prayer.

Some frugal advisors will say that it's cheaper and smarter to rent. I don't agree. I watched rents soar and house sales double in just a few years. I felt my face flush and my heart flutter nervously when I read the current state of the real estate market. But I kept to my belief that we should buy a house with a mortgage so low that we could pay it on one income, and if something happened to the breadwinner's job, we could work flipping burgers and bagging groceries and still pay the mortgage easily.

I rented for 27 years of my life, and I always had decent places with good landlords, but I know that most places don't have rent control and not all landlords are generous nor work with a tenant. If you are right on the edge with your finances and it comes time to resign the rental lease and, say, the landlord decides to get in on the new higher rents and profits and raises your rent a couple hundred or more, what will you do? If you decide to move, you need to come up with thousands of dollars in 30 days for first, last, and security deposit, not to mention moving costs, a moving truck, and so on. Scary stuff.

For me, buying a house meant that I would never have to worry about my rent going up or the landlord deciding to sell the property and having to go through the scenario I just described. We owned the place and that felt like stability. We could also paint the rooms any color, plant as much food as we wanted, put in fruit trees, put in solar panels, and utilize every inch of space to work for us.

We have purchased two houses in the last five years. Both houses were not pretty to the unimaginative eye and both houses needed a lot of work. However, both houses had "good bones." They were solid and with some elbow grease and TLC, they became charming homes. Both houses were affordable because they weren't popular or in the perfect neighborhoods. They were old and had old wiring and needed sprucing up. Not everyone can look at a grungy house and see the vision of what it could be with some work.

The second house was a bit more because it was in a lovely area with charming old towns. The mortgage was higher, but it was the same amount as we had paid in rent for years when we made very little money.

After reading *Evicted*, I felt so much gratitude for having shelter. Our roof doesn't leak, the foundation is solid, and most of the house is insulated, which is fantastic for a 120-year-old house. We have a huge yard and that means we can plant a lot of food trees and have a large garden.

It didn't matter that the rooms are small. Look at European or Asian homes. They are tiny. Only Americans feel like they need more house than they use, and studies show that people only use about 600 square feet of their 2,500 square foot house. Imagine how much land could have been spared? People could have smaller homes and more yards to grow gardens, flowers, and trees.

I read a comment from a channel about poor man's soup. The subscriber was thanking the channel for teaching them to cook for little money. The channel had helped them get through a rough time when they had no home or work. Now, he proudly claimed, they had two great jobs and a bigger house. That is a sign of progress and success in our society. Bigger house, a bigger car. Whether we need it or not, whether we use it all or not, this is what we are proud about, never mind that we both must work full-time jobs to afford the bigger house and we are never home to enjoy the bigger home. Most people struggle to pay the mortgage on a big house. Most families are just one paycheck away from losing it all.

Maybe a smaller house and cash-paid used car in exchange for more stability and security?

Our house has three bedrooms and two bathrooms in 1,100 square feet. That also includes a laundry and pantry area. For four people and three dogs, it is cozy and perfect. It's still too much to clean. I would be exhausted keeping a large house clean and organized.

We rented out the first house, only because we were having no luck selling it. But it turned into great luck because we sold it a year later for much more than we ever thought possible. We sold it to a small family who fell in love with it, and, according to my neighbors, they are gardening and adoring the house just as we once did.

Because I'd read *Evicted* and had a new perspective on the importance of having a home, we took the profit from the sale of that property and paid off almost half of this current home. Before the check was handed to us, we dreamt big. We talked of getting a new car, maybe a used RV to travel sometimes (which we don't do), and possibly doing all sorts of home improvements. But the day the check was in our hands we quickly sent the money off to our mortgage company. We don't have an RV or a new car, but we have a small mortgage once again. We are closer to owning our house outright.

To have a house you can afford is a blessing, even if it's not so pretty. A scrub brush, soap, and some warm colors in a paint can will fix that.

We used leftover paint from our old house along with paint some friends and neighbors had given us. We mixed paint and had a good time covering bland walls in a variety of colors including yellow, pumpkin orange, various blues, lime, and pink. We redid the floor with bamboo, only because it was on enormous clearance at The Home Depot and was less expensive than the cheapest flooring. We hung old curtains I had saved from years ago that I bought at Big Lots. Our used furniture was too big and bulky for this house, so I scrubbed and bleached it and gave it all away on Craigslist. I then found replacements for free or cheap on Craigslist. I found things on the street for free. In our neighborhoods, we all put things out on the street with free signs. I've gotten everything from dressers and clean loveseats, to half-dead houseplants, and even a new espresso maker still in the box for free.

When it comes to decorating my little home, I'm not too proud to rummage through a box on the street marked FREE.

Quarantines and Our Present Reality

Since the quarantines, many of us have gotten used to being isolated. I know that some shutdowns are happening again here and there. I can't use the library right now because it's shut down again.

I won't say what I think about the world right now and I can't predict anything or advise anyone on how to recreate a life after or during such events. I will say that for me and my family, we just got busy.

When the lockdowns began, we planted an orchard and started a garden plot. We painted, fixed floors, and nested. We worked hard through the first year and I had way too much going on which was partly good but partly led to burnout.

We have lost some loved ones. Not physically in death, or through fights or disagreements. It's just what is happening now with all the division of ideas and thoughts on how things should be handled. Some people are terrified of COVID-19, and some are not. We are not and never were. We had it and got through it, and I have absolute confidence in our immune system. But others don't feel so confident and prefer to socially distance themselves or remain in quarantine. We just respect that.

I have found that we are attracting new friends and have deepened our bonds with them. I feel like our social life is better now than ever before, but moderate at the same time, and I like that too. I love people but only in small doses. I'm 51 years old and I cherish my time and privacy more each day. I'm busy with projects and routines, and socializing can be a lot of work. Sometimes I have the best conversations at the grocery store and then we part ways after having had a good chat for 10 minutes or so over bell peppers. That is my favorite. I enjoy the person so much for that moment and then I leave them there at the store and go on with life.

When we experienced some lonely seasons, I began focusing on making our home and land a sanctuary and focused on creating a Zen-like life. I have no interest in becoming a nun or immersing myself in the Zen or Buddhist life, but I do love studying them, watching them in documentaries, and taking parts of that life to apply to my days.

Building a sanctuary in your home is an emotional thing. It is the building of a space that is pleasing to the senses and feels safe and nurturing. It is a place you want to be often.

In our home, we have painted all the rooms warm or cool colors. Two bedrooms are blue and I'm not crazy about it. I've planned to paint one a warm pumpkin and the other a light milk chocolate. I'm always working on the house, changing spaces around with different furnishings, or repainting in colors that are more soothing and healing.

Our home is filled with comfortable, overstuffed sofas and super soft beds. We have piles of comforters and fleece blankets for chilly winters along with fluffy pillows, and yes, some are lumpy. There are vibrant colors everywhere, lush plants, a thick area rug, piles of good books, and movies to get lost in. I have a small library and in it, you can find books to inspire you, heal you, entertain you, and teach you.

My kitchen is very clean, but the counters are always busy with containers, jars, and scattered flour. The oven is often preheating, and there is usually an open cookbook on the table. In the morning, you can always smell homemade bread toasting. Other days it's granola slowly baking in the oven, and a roast is almost tender and moist around the time my husband gets home from work.

I only have a small stack of cookbooks, but they are all about some form of scratch-cooking. I had all the fancy *Joy of Cooking* and other such cookbooks, but I donated them for an animal shelter fundraiser, and when I decided that getting offline might be in my future and I wouldn't be able to browse my favorite websites such as Allrecipes.com or Tasteofhome.com, I found used copies of my favorite books, such as the aforementioned *Make-A-Mix* series. I love these books so much and will never donate these kitchen gems.

The other day we went to a group healing done by Tibetan monks. I have to say, I haven't been the same. This was our third day with the monks and their presence is so soothing that we just kept showing up. The group healing was deep, and I decided that when I walked out of the small building, I would do everything in my power every day and every moment to *not* go back to my old ways of things, nor to my old thinking.

It is work, I'll say that, but it is possible to heal yourself daily and commit to a journey of self-love and transformation. It is inside and outside work. We heal our thinking, and it changes our feelings, then our vibration, and then we slowly begin to see our outer world (our reality) begin to change in wondrous ways.

Sometimes it's small shifts, and then bigger and more frequent shifts, until you wake up one day very happy about silly things like fresh coffee and maybe a new creamer you found at the store last night and you can't wait to try it. Then you can't wait to take that steaming, hot, creamy, sweet cup of coffee and sit down at your laptop and type up all your thoughts and feelings. You love the way the morning sun comes through your window, you can hear the birds outside, and it makes you feel like the world is safe and there is love.

A sanctuary is safe and quiet. Ours is not quiet but it's safe. We don't allow news. I haven't watched the news consciously in years. I would sometimes get caught up in a headline on Yahoo Mail when I would clear out my inbox and it'd pop up. Once, when I was sick, I foolishly watched the news and political dramas and I found my mental well-being diminished within days, maybe hours. I noticed that I felt so unnerved and frightened, so overwhelmed by it all that I didn't know how long I wanted to stay on this planet, except I have kids to stay for. I also noticed that it took a few weeks to detox but the minute I decided to shut it off and didn't go back, the healing began.

I don't watch disturbing things or read disturbing books. I did get into a psycho thriller recently, *The Silent Patient*, but it was more mystery, and a shockingly good whodunit, rather than emotional.

I don't listen to angry music either.

Some naysayers claim you can't live in a bubble or stick your head in the sand. I ask, "Why not?" You can, and still make positive changes in this world. I live in a bubble now and it is good for me and my children, my husband, and even the dogs, who pick up on all our energy. I am so ignorant that I am surprised by things like the library closing again.

I still vote for good causes, I put my money into positive things and support good companies. I care deeply about the environment, and I do what I can as an individual. We clean up trash, plant flowers for bees, feed birds, and create natural beauty where we live. We fix up ugly houses and help improve neighborhoods with that one act. I support businesses and companies that care about the environment and their employees. We try to reduce our waste and plastic all the time. We fail often but we also get a little better as we go.

The metaphysical belief is that we can't fight for causes. We must reflect on the good, lead by example, and be a shining light.

Think of the vegans back in the day when they would throw fake blood on people wearing fur coats. They were passionate, yes, but it didn't help the cause much. The action made them look like crazy people and turned other people off. Now vegans promote their cause in fun, creative, playful ways. The way to everyone's heart is through their stomach and vegans are cooking up amazing foods that include meat and dairy alternatives. They are making fantastic faux leather, and well, they are just making the vegan lifestyle look so fun and sparkly. The movement has grown by some insane leaps and bounds. Even some people that aren't devoted vegans are doing it part-time now. We even tried going vegan on and off for a few years and it was the most fun I ever had in the kitchen, veganizing everything. I still make a ton of vegan foods, despite introducing meat into our diet again. But we don't eat meat the way we used to. We use meat as a condiment or for flavoring instead of as the star of the meal.

We can change the world in ways that are filled with sparkle and soft warmth. We can put our attention on the good and expand it. We can quietly turn away from what we don't support anymore.

This brings me to our days as consumers. We are trying very hard to not shop from the big box stores. I don't hate them; I just think they are getting too greedy, and I want to support our little town and keep it going. I also think some of these big companies could do much more in order to be leaders in environmental change and support their employees, making happier workplaces and supporting the towns they settle in instead of putting everyone out of business the way Walmart has had a reputation for doing for decades now.

It's not easy. Places like Walmart and Amazon make it so easy to shop and they have the customer service down like a science. You want something and a click or two later, it's at your door. Hard to turn away from that relationship. But the shopping trend is a black hole. You just need to shut it down and not look back.

So, yes, you can change the world from your porch, that is my point. And yes, you can live a Zen-like life. Sometimes you do have to go out and mix with the world but if you have a haven to return to, you won't mind as much.

Think of the monks and how they live in sanctuaries. They come to town and travel to cities to reach out to others, to heal them with their presence and prayers, but then they return to this sanctuary that heals them and has order and structure, silence, and peace.

I'm fascinated by them. I glean what I can bring into my reality and over the years I keep building in tiny acts.

Monks have their sanctuaries, and sometimes they are lovely places in nature. They are simple, clean, and have some sweet decor such as statues and art. They have the same routine daily. Wake up early, meditate, make the morning meal, eat in silence, and do chores such as wash floors and sweep courtyards. Every group is different. Some monks go out with their begging bowls and collect the meal from the villagers and then cook and eat together. Some have gardens, harvest food, and cook in the sanctuary.

I realized that I could take what I like and feels right, and apply it to our lives.

How To Cook Your Life is such a good documentary on food, baking, and our inner selves. It's about all the factory, processed foods we consume without soul or nutrients and what it does to our bodies and emotions. It's about making our food from scratch that is clean, healthy, made with love and time, and how that food feeds us in more ways than just our physical hunger.

I wanted a Zen-like life ever since a friend commented one day. I was stressed about something not so important, and she said, "What do you have to worry about? You have this Zen-like life!" And it dawned on me that I do have this Zen-like life, but I was making things unnecessarily busy and stressful. I could remake it all and have that blissful and dreamy life she was suggesting that I already had. That was a couple of years ago, and I've been weeding and planting this garden ever since. Pulling the Internet plug was the biggest and most brilliant move that has sped up the process.

I also find myself feeling emotionally exhausted with the complicated books and movies or too much work at once.

I can only look at what is in front of me right now. Be present now. I need entertainment that is not complicated, and I love to laugh.

We have an old radio in the living room that I found at Goodwill and a small radio in the kitchen that I found on the street. Both get the local stations. They aren't Pandora, that is for sure, but I enjoy the catchy, cheesy songs from the '80s and '90s. The local station plays blues and such sometimes and I love that.

Without the Internet, I can't have whatever I want when I want it. Nothing is at my fingertips now. I just enjoy what presents itself and I'm thrilled when something delightful shows up.

Life gets simpler and easier each day.

Chapter 8

Daily Life In The "Other" World

There is always the concern that withdrawing from the world will bring loneliness and isolation. I have found the opposite to be true. We must go places to get Wi-Fi and now that I'm rested, or decompressing, people are flooding in.

This morning I had two phone conversations with two different girlfriends. One is Dawn, from *Centsible Living with Money Mom* on YouTube, whom I met because she started a channel around the time I started my first channel. We became friends and she taught me how to monetize and start the Amazon affiliate program. She and I loved to talk shop and we kept each other motivated. She has become a very good friend over the past year and we do coffee chats almost daily. It is a wonderful thing to have that girlfriend whom you chat with most mornings over a coffee and get each other motivated for the day.

The other person is a neighbor I had back in the days of living on the river in the fruit orchard. She reminded me that despite my glorifying those days, we still had our complaints. Of course, there is always something to rant about, right? Now that I don't work on the channel as often, I torture everyone separately with speeches on the importance of cooking from scratch among other homemaking things. She said prices have gone up and I replied, "Make it from scratch." I'm not saying prices haven't gone up, but my grocery bill is lower than ever. It all depends on how you cook, what you buy, and how you buy it. Do you buy premade or bulk foods you make at home from a cookbook? Do you buy any produce you want to eat, or do you go for what is in season and less expensive?

Then yet another friend came over for coffee and we talked as fast as we could over second cups of coffee for two hours. She's worried over the world's predicaments, and she experiences depression and anger. I can't tell people to shut it off and forget about it because that is often met with hostility. I just sit with them, and I feel compassion for their pain. I've been there.

The boys asked for the evening menu and I had pulled out some ribs yesterday. We have no barbecue sauce and I have no desire to leave the house. Yesterday I sat in our truck in the library parking lot doing some work, so today, we stayed home.

I still have data, so I searched and found a fantastic recipe on Allrecipes.com and wrote it down so next month when I have very little data, I don't have to look these things up. I do need to find a good ketchup recipe. I don't think there is one in my many cookbooks, at least I haven't come across one. I will also look up mayonnaise. I have a low-calorie recipe, but the last thing I desire is low-calorie mayo.

I whipped up the barbecue sauce and I have to say, it was quite pleasing. The house was looking disheveled. I set the timer for an hour and a half and with the boys' help, we cleaned and picked up the house. I was inspired by my girlfriend's talk about how she's been getting her house in order just by putting things in their place. Make a place for everything and put it there. I quickly reorganized my library and put all the books that were stacked everywhere back on the shelves. I folded and put away all the extra afghans, moved out all the furniture, and vacuumed everywhere. I heated some wax scents for a bit to give the house a nice smell. I had a roast cooking in the oven. By the time Bali got home, the house was clean and neat and he was greeted by the smell of a delicious dinner.

We had some good movies and books coming from the library and we got very excited. Before we would just have the TV running mindlessly and barely pay attention. Now we look on the library website to see what is coming and we are eager for Bali's arrival with the bagful of goodies.

We have turned back the hands of time and gone right back to the '70s in some ways, but still benefit from the modern joys. Sending my tax lady all the paperwork through my phone instead of faxing and scanning away was refreshing. Having a DVD player as our only source of entertainment yet having the libraries be filled with such great, new movies and books nowadays is a dream.

I love the modern world in many ways. What we decide to get rid of and what we decide to keep is our choice. I can say no to the Internet and watch DVDs and listen to the local radio instead. I can keep the modern washer, dryer, vacuum, and bread machine for the lazy days. Or I can make bread by hand, hang laundry outside, and sweep the entire house when I'm in the mood for some physical therapy.

Chapter 9

Routines and Rituals for Mental Well-Being

It seems that everyone I meet has some mental health condition and/or their children have been diagnosed with conditions as well. It also seems to me that most people are stressed, constantly worried, depressed, and/or addicted to something to force calmness, sleep, or false joy or contentment.

Everybody's story is different, and everybody will argue their case. It's not for me to say or judge. But what I truly, honestly think is going on in most cases is that people have too much time on their hands and life has been set up for absolute inactivity and isolation.

Look at the newer developments. Towns used to be small buildings along the main street lined with trees. Neighborhoods were built around the town, and you could walk everywhere. You could walk to the post office or bakery. There would be a movie theater on Main Street along with cafes, pubs, and coffee shops around it. Things were set up for the community.

People had to do things physically back in the day. Laundry was done by hand or wringer washer, which required hands-on work and focus. You raked leaves, swept the driveway, walked everywhere, and used brooms. If you were out in the country, you woke up with the sun and went down with the sun. You lived naturally with the seasons, planting in spring, tending to things in the summer, harvesting and canning in the fall, and resting and planning in the winter. People kept to themselves except for Sunday and then everyone gathered for some spiritual food and community, sharing after church meals and gathering. Harvest time was a very social time as well with everyone gathering to help husk, pick, can, and such.

Mothers were so busy baking and cooking everything from scratch because stores didn't start making an appearance until the early 1900s. They were mending and scrubbing and had their kitchen gardens out the back door. Everything was done by hand. Kids played or helped their parents all day outside.

Then there was information and gossip. They may have gone to town once a week or once every few months and heard the local gossip. Maybe the mailman would make it out to their place once a week and bring the local news. But you only heard the local news unless a war was going on and then it may be a bit more global.

Today we are bombarded with information from the minute we are conscious in the morning to the time we fall asleep at night. We spend all day multi-tasking between our computers and iPhones, scrolling, commenting, watching and posting, and checking and rechecking and doing more scrolling. Our phones ding and ping to let us know every time someone has posted or emailed or farted. We take in all sorts of news and media and hundreds of opinions an hour. And we try to process all that every day, every hour.

New towns are not built for people or communities at all. Look at Los Angeles or Sacramento. They are built by developers that build things for money, not creative expression or charm or out of love. They build the towns for cars. And consumption. The main street is no longer two lanes, it's 10 lanes wide. It is a highway so we can get as many cars on there as possible. We have strip malls with huge parking lots and huge buildings so we can pack as many shoppers and consumers in as possible.

Neighborhoods are full of huge houses that are all the same color, with no expression of personality, unless everyone's personality is tan. They sit on small lawns and neglected backyards. They sit empty with double garages for more cars but no porches for sitting with a cup of coffee. The houses are empty all day because they cost so much that both owners of the house need to work to cover the mortgage of this lonely, bland shell. Interestingly, people buy huge houses for space, but no one's home. Why not live in a camper? Most people seem to only need a kitchen, bathroom, and bed.

Neighborhoods are surrounded by walls and built so that you must drive to the house and drive to work because there is no train station like in the olden days when a family was lucky to have one car and the husband took a train to work. You drive to the market, to the multiplex theater, to the gym to get in that hour of exercise so you can sit around the rest of the day and scroll and post things and then take a pill at night because your mind won't calm down enough for you to sleep and you just don't understand why this is.

But here is the good news! Developers and residents are looking at this and realizing that this model hasn't worked for decades. In 2008 during the big recession, there were news clips on how unsustainable suburbia was. People that were forced to drive everywhere went into a downward financial spiral when gas prices went up. There are lists of other issues as well, but I'll just say that they are starting to change things. They are putting in bike lanes and walking paths and designing with more trees and more of a community feel or putting in Town Squares.

There are a couple of positive and interesting channels on YouTube that discuss this: *Freethink* and *Not Just Bikes*. The latter explores our car-obsessed America and Canada and how they have built new cities and neighborhoods that are purposely made to increase car usage. Many cities and towns are taking back their streets. And the old grid system of building a town so it is walkable is coming back.

In the meantime, how about returning to some old-fashioned living? Can we change things so we can live at a slower pace but have more physical or hands-on work?

I find that the less I must connect myself to the outside world and the more I focus on the natural order of things such as rising with the sun, going with the seasons, being present in each moment, focusing on my family day to day, and being present in our home or our garden, the more peace I feel. The more I make everything from scratch and sweep with a broom, water my porch plants from a bucket of tub water, and do my daily rituals slowly and with full attention, the more content and accomplished I feel.

This morning we did some homeschooling. The boys work from books and focus on reading, writing, and math. When it comes to science, social studies, or history, they can choose whatever interests them. We just work on the basic subjects daily. We also do piano exercises and once a week the music teacher comes to our home to teach them. He is young and creative and when they do the lessons, they don't do boring scales and songs from an old piano book. They play around with sounds and songs. They try to play songs they love. Sam loves Dolly Parton's 9 to 5, so they play with that. Arjan is into more haunting and bizarre music he finds in dinosaur videos. I bought them an electric piano that looks and sounds just like a grand piano except that it has so many sounds, instruments, and songs built-in so they can play the traditional piano or get wild and fun. The more they are allowed to play and try new things the more they sit down and play around daily and the more they love their lessons.

I'd say we spend huge amounts of our day doing what we enjoy. I make homemaking into something healing and creative by focusing on how I feel when I clean our home and especially after the house is fresh and in order. Bali and I grow flowers and food and it feels like big investments are being grown and tended to. Arjan has self-educated himself on so many subjects I would need a book to list it all. Sam helps me in the kitchen. We create dishes together and he likes to help me keep our pantry organized and neat.

I brew coffee in a little stovetop espresso maker each morning and foam my cream in a small, plug-in milk frother. I love mornings. I turn on the heat and give thanks that I don't have to build a fire instead. I have lived like that through my childhood and in my adult years briefly, so I know what it's like. But now I press a button and the heat gushes through the vents and heats the whole house quickly. I turn on the pot on the stove and press the button on the milk frother for my hot, whipped cream. Then I go about opening curtains and feeding dogs, turning on the radio to something pleasant for the morning music. When the espresso pot bubbles, I can smell that fresh coffee drifting through the house. Ah, and then we have warmth, freshly brewed coffee, and maybe some bluegrass on the radio - the mountain life.

I have found that starting the main meal for the day early in the morning is wise. When doing scratch cooking, I need to be on top of it and make food early on. Maybe it's a slow cooker dinner that takes hours or I need to make bread and it needs to rise a few times before going in the oven. So, I have my coffee, chat on the phone with my earpiece, and my phone in my apron pocket so my hands are free to work and prepare for the day.

We eat meals at the table and talk or we enjoy being in the living room during cold winter days because it's filled with comfortable furniture and a heater. The radio may be on, and we read and draw. I have no talent for drawing, so I color in the grown-up coloring books. Or I may go to my room where I've created a little writing nook with a free, white desk and a thrifted lamp with a free lampshade I found on the side of the road. There is a cork board that was also free, a framed fairy card that was sent to me by a subscriber, a plant that was given to me by a neighbor's friend years ago, a Himalayan lamp, and a buddha. I have put up a poster of NaNoWriMo, a dream board I made before moving up here, a great photo of the boys, and a small painting of Jesus laughing. I have stacks of my books on paperback to remind me of the work I have accomplished and books I'm reading. I sit here with my coffee and write like crazy.

There are evening rituals of cooking and eating the main meal and talking to the husband about projects. I feed the dogs and take Molly for a walk around the neighborhoods. When I return, if I didn't play with the old dogs in the morning, I play with them then. They love chasing after a ball and we have a long driveway so I'm able to exercise them well. I like to do it in the morning, so they are calm and lay about the porch in the sun. They sleep better at night and don't get up at ungodly hours to go outside to pee or sniff out a night critter. They are old but healthy because of exercise and a good diet.

Sometimes, when it's warm, we will pack finger foods, bars, fruit, and water and have our breakfast in the forest. We walk up to the park forest and sit on a fallen log and have our morning meal and enjoy the sounds and smells of the woods.

Sometimes we walk around town and play in a very old cemetery where the first pioneers are buried. We can go to the park or ride bikes on the fairgrounds. Everything is free and out in the fresh air.

In the summer, I love watering by hand. I just enjoy being out in the morning hearing the squirrels and birds and feeling the sun warm me up. I love to look at my trees and see how much bigger they get each year. Every year the garden has a little more success as the soil improves and every year the trees get stronger.

The other thing we do is walk everywhere for almost everything we can think up. A small trip to the store or the local library. A dog is a great way to stay on a daily walking schedule. Molly will whine and give me those sweet brown eyes around the time we should be walking until I can't bear it and off we go. Many times, in the evenings, we find the best free things. One evening, I found a nice little painting of the forest and a little green snifter glass for Sam to use as his play glass. He loves drinking out of teacups and wine glasses. A couple of days later we found a big watercolor that looks great in the living room. Then a standing lamp with a sweet yellow shade and light green trim and a frill. The next evening with Molly and Sam, we found canned food items. We took some of the canned tuna and chicken. Another day it was a nice, small coffee table that fits under my window better than the round table I had. I then put some things out on our street for free in exchange.

I've put so many good things out on the street for free that I have no shame in dragging things home from other streets. It seems we all do this around here. Sometimes, I take it to the thrift store or put it up on Craigslist but putting it in front of my house seems to be the most efficient and the neighbors get the first choice. When I see things out on the street, I don't get embarrassed, I get excited. What is better than finding a new painting or piece of furniture for free?!

I don't just drag anything home. It should be an item that has caught my eye, is clean and charming, and will go well in the house. Something we will use and enjoy. At this point, we could have completely decorated our house for free with what we find on the street and what is offered on Craigslist.

Chapter 10

A New Way of Spending Money or Thinking About It

This lifestyle change is still new. One night, after realizing that I would have to let go of another job that brings in money, I sat down to write out a new budget. I spent the next day calling, emailing, and just getting into my accounts and canceling anything that wasn't a bill for shelter, water, gas, solar, or garbage. I found old, unused envelopes and labeled them Gas, Groceries, Vet Bills, Dental, Car Repair, Entertainment, and Home Improvements. I had seen a woman do what she called "cash stuffing" her envelopes monthly and keeping a tally. I now recognize the psychology behind this. We have savings, but we don't dare touch it, if at all possible. If we have envelopes for each item, we feel easy about using them. After all, we have saved for that item specifically.

We went from needing $3,100 plus to make the bills, down to $2,482. But this is tight, and we will have to be careful and attentive. We are now living below our monthly income. I felt so relieved and joyful after I created our new budget.

I felt joyful because we are free of the money trap. We can live on very little, and I can focus on my sons as they grow so fast, alleviating stress from missing these moments with them. I feel huge amounts of guilt not being present in mind and spirit when I'm with them because my mind is on filming or what I'm going to film or what I did film. I enjoyed the work, but it consumes me and there is no being present in the now with this work as I was in my head pondering what to create next. I couldn't even read a book without thinking about what I would say about it or if I'd make a video on the subject. There was no being present in any moment.

I am joyful because now I can focus on my homemaking, which I adore. I feel great accomplishment in making food, treats, and condiments from scratch. It feels like a craft to have homemade ketchup, mayonnaise, and pickles on the table. I feel like I'm making art every day.

The grocery budget is purposely small at the moment. I'm challenged by it in a very fun way. I think differently about what I buy now. This is just until we get a few things accomplished, and then if I need to increase the grocery envelope, I will.

I make a list of what we need for the next shopping trip, and I must rethink items. I can no longer justify expensive monk fruit or all organics. I used to buy store bread, and not just any bread - fancy Dave's Killer Bread and other pre-made foods and snacks, chips, and bars. Three hundred dollars won't stretch far with those items on the list.

I will buy regular sugar as honey is very expensive. We used to buy the cheap, large tin of honey but even that surpasses a couple of dollars for sugar. I buy milk instead of cream. I buy big bags of peanuts in the shell to make peanut butter as that is far cheaper than a jar of the store-bought stuff. I have buckets of flour for making white bread and wheat bread. I will make many bean dishes flavoring them this way and that, some with cheese, some with tortillas. I buy whole chickens and ground beef and they last weeks. We use the meat for flavoring. We used to be more plant-based but we go off and on. We crave meat and cheese and then we go back to tofu and lentils. I loved vegan eating; my family was tired of it. But eating meat and cheese has increased the grocery budget. I can do four chickens and four packets of beef. That is for the month. I can't compromise on grass-fed or hormone-free meats. I can buy produce from the Clean 15 list and save money for the produce that must be organic.

We don't need fancy fruits or vegetables. We can store up large bags of potatoes, carrots, and cabbage. Bananas, apples, and oranges provide plenty of vitamins. It doesn't have to be boring. I will admit that it made me a little nervous to work with such simple foods. However, there is a fantastic channel, *The Perfect Home*, on YouTube. She works with just these foods and makes amazing dishes. She uses meat and cheese very sparingly. She uses flour liberally with the vegetables. She gave me the idea to make handheld pies from leftovers.

Today we had leftover boiled potatoes and peas that no one wanted a thing to do with. So, I cooked up some bacon pieces I bought in bulk for very little and I added the leftover peas, potatoes, and gravy and made a batch of pizza dough. With all this, I made handheld pies, or empanadas. What was once bland food my family balked at, was now this delicious meal they loved.

I almost feel as if I'm earning a college degree here. I feel so good about not wasting food, and so artistic for whipping something up out of very few ingredients.

I enjoy this work, this figuring out of things. This is but a game that helps us live more humbly and be present in what matters: family and a craft. The craft that I want to focus on as my side thing is my writing. My writing goes well with my work of nesting and tending to the family. Homemaking and writing enjoy each other.

I will no longer buy anything. I need nothing. My family needs nothing. They need attention and nurturing and wholesome foods. Like our garden, we need fresh air, sun, and nature. We need play, art, books, music, and movies. All free things. Everything we do every day is free and richer than going out to eat or shopping. We have friends over and we visit friends. We help them work and we drink espresso drinks and talk over each other in excitement.

I'm careful about who I spend time with. So many people are upset right now. They may have a good reason but when you study history and go back thousands of years and beyond, you will realize that human problems, corrupt governments, dynasties, and injustices are nothing new. You can encourage the positive by placing your attention and support on the good. I no longer want to hear negativity or be a part of it. I love people, but I find myself upset all over again when I sit with them for too long.

I prefer uplifting conversations, and solution based ones. I love conversations on what we can do to be happier and share that with others. I can't save this country, and I certainly can't save another where I don't reside. I can share a meal, rescue an animal, send some money now and then, sign a petition, and stop shopping with a corporation I don't agree with. We do what we can in our home and yard to add beauty and provide sanctuaries for nature and weary souls.

Monks are peaceful. They change the vibration of a place, a town, and people, lifting them up with their presence alone. Work on yourself and you begin the change the world hungers for. Being a better person is often a gift to many.

Love is free, time is precious. I am joyful to live this way, so I have this time.

I do believe most of us have to go through the phases of working too much, spending too often, maybe incurring some debt or even a lot of debt, and stressful living. This way we can fall in love with the other way of living. We have been to the dark side, and we have learned that there is never enough money, success, or power to fill us up the way quiet moments with loved ones does. None of that provides the sweet feeling that getting our hands in the soil to plant fresh food or drinking coffee in the morning does. We can appreciate slowing down and enjoying the simple things.

It takes time to get used to having very little money. It is not a sacrifice, and you don't have to suffer once you learn to work with your budget. It takes time to get used to not shopping senselessly. It takes time to learn the art of frugality. It takes time to see the payoffs and have small and great success with the budget and find that the thrill of saving on some item or getting a great deal is far more delicious than spending on things that you don't have in your hand the next day. Spending money on a yarn clearance and having a bag full of yarn that you can make warm scarves or blankets with is far more satisfying than an expensive dinner out. The dinner may not be that satisfying and is over in less than 30 minutes, with nothing to show for it.

There is shopping for perishables and there is investing in items that serve you for years. Going to dinner is perishable. Buying a Berkey water filter is something that serves you for ages. Buying a cookbook will save you thousands over a short period of time.

The amount we spend eating out is enough to fill a couple of pantry shelves and some freezer space and can feed my family for a week or so. Choosing groceries over dinner means I don't have to work all the hustles to put the money back in the bank. It means I can live a slow life.

It's not forever. It's a season. There are times to thrive and spend, go out, and shop it up; and there are times to settle in and keep that wallet closed tight.

I was reading through my old copy of the ten-pound *The Complete Tightwad Gazette*, and I read a letter from a reader who spoke of her early years of marriage and how lean it was. She would hand wash clothes and hang them over the tub or out on the banisters and sit out there reading on the steps to make sure no one stole the clothes. They only had $17 a week for groceries (this was in 1970) but if they went even a penny over, they put something back. She sat in the dark at night to save on lights (her husband worked nights). They bought no clothes, books, or magazines.

But it was all temporary. Over time, things get better or change. Economies rise and fall and rise again. Jobs are lost and new ones are found. Earning an education or learning new trades changes our income bracket.

My favorite topic is pursuing a dream and being okay with being broke because you know it is only for a small time. Those broke years are filled with faith and ambition. It is a fun challenge with a bright future.

When our dream was to move up here, I did all sorts of small and big things to save a dollar here, a handful of change there. I would empty vacuum bags over and over to make them last. Now I own a bagless vacuum. I would recycle my coffee grounds by using the grounds from the first brew and a little bit of fresh grounds to the pot the next day. This does make your coffee supply last. I still water down my dish soap and sometimes the shampoo too, because it is so condensed.

One year, I saved all my cans from our holiday meals and used them for my plant starts in the spring instead of buying small containers. I learned this in Connie Hultquist's book, *Dear Kitchen Saints*. She talked of the Depression era mothers and how they saved cans to plant seeds in, then put them in sunny windows throughout the house. People didn't have greenhouses back then. They didn't have nurseries to buy pots or starts. They didn't have money. They were creative. People had to find ways to make it. Box stores and supermarkets didn't exist back in the early 1900s. Markets came about shortly after the 1900s but they weren't located everywhere.

No matter how broke we are or how limited things are for us, it can never compare to the Depression era, or to other countries where some people live in shelters built of scraps and tarps and have no toilets or running water.

I used to read books about the Depression era, and I've watched documentaries on other countries. I used to take cruises and see for myself such poverty in Mexican towns. It was shocking. I can't read or watch these things anymore because they make me too sad, but I have enormous gratitude for our running water, a proper toilet, lights, heat, and air conditioning. We eat well; sometimes too well and too much. We have a strong house that doesn't leak in the winter. We have land to grow food or raise chickens if there is a need. We even have space for a pig, a goat, rabbits...

I can get greedy and dissatisfied like everyone else. It is, sadly, human nature and something that we must frequently purge ourselves of. I do it by remembering others that have truly rough lives or our grandparents that struggled through the wars and poor times. Then I remember that our lives are very easy and luxurious compared to that.

All it takes is losing everything and winding up on the street trying to survive to appreciate the simple hot meal or a dry place to live.

I don't mean to be dark at all. I just think that we should look at the simple things in our lives and be content *without* needing much more and we will have a lot of happiness. We can live on less money and have more time for pursuing dreams or being with family.

Chapter 11

A Normal Day for Unplugged Folk

I rose early this morning. I had strange dreams, so my thoughts were not very pleasant. The first of the morning thoughts must be positive and pleasant. It wasn't going well so I got up and got busy. That is the solution to negative mind flow. Get busy doing something productive. Everyone remained snuggled in and sleeping well.

I turned on the heat and began pulling back the living room drapes and kitchen curtains to let in the morning sun. I set the stovetop percolator and espresso pot on the stove to brew and turned on the local radio station, which was playing some bluegrass, much to my delight. I loved how the morning felt. The house was warming up and cozy with the sun filling the rooms. I left the bedroom drapes closed so my family would sleep as long as possible. We stayed up late, they needed sleep, and I love those quiet moments to myself to greet and prepare for the day.

The house is warm and sunny, the smell of fresh coffee fills the kitchen, the bluegrass is playing, making me feel all the parts of a mountain life morning. The dishes were washed and dried in the rack, and the counters were washed. I even scoured the top of the stove before I began brewing the coffee. I remember Clara, from *Great Depression Cooking* on YouTube, talking about her mother having a thing about a clean stove. She would clean the stove before cooking and she would clean her sister's stove when visiting because she couldn't stand how dirty it was.

I started the flour and yeast for baking bread and poured myself an espresso with my frothed cream. I set up Bali's water and coffee as he was up now.

Once everyone is up it gets busy with all sorts of things. The dogs need to be fed, and Sam likes tea and oatmeal, so I set about making a pot of green tea and a small pot of oatmeal with walnut milk and raisins. I read that children can have one cup of green tea daily. Green tea has so many benefits. We found three boxes of brown rice Genmaicha tea and we drink it daily now.

I had the best chat with my friend Dawn this morning. We have coffee and talk about the happiest and most positive things. Mostly we talk about how to improve ourselves and bring in more joy and less worry or fear.

I was thinking about Beyonce's song *Run The World (Girls)*. I was worried about the world this morning; this still happens, and I need to shake it off. For some odd reason, the song came to mind, but I replaced the word with fear and greed. "Who runs the world? Fear!" "Who runs the world? Greed!"

Sam is obsessed with nuclear bombs and worries. It is a sick, insane, and unacceptable thing that we even have them, still. They should have been dismantled and banned globally from the start when it was realized how horrific they are. The fact that we even continue to build more when a fraction of them would end all life as we know it shows how insane and fearful mankind is. People should NOT live in this fear, children should NEVER have to worry about these things. I never told Sam about bombs. Kids find it on YouTube. Another reason to have canceled the Internet is so I can retrieve my kid's childhood and monitor things carefully.

But after a full morning of cooking and music, warmth and sunlight, and a happy family, I soon forgot my worries from earlier.

I'm diligently working from the pantry. We have barely purchased groceries this month. Maybe some cream, a bag of apples, bananas, and onions. Nothing much and we have had delicious meals and treats made from pantry storage and scratch cooking. But now it's time to do a little shopping. We need produce, white flour, sugar and such.

I was gung-ho to go shopping at first, but I was enjoying my comfy pajamas and a second cup of coffee. I wanted to get back to this book and then Bali brought in the mail and the *How To Cook Your Life* documentary came! I just wanted to put it on and sit on the couch with the heater on and work.

I made a clear and organized grocery list for the man and boys. I went over it with my eldest son, Arjan. It sounded more like a complicated science project. "Get the non-GMO popcorn. Yes, the kernels, not the microwaveable kind. That's just junk and it's expensive. Any vegetables with a star mean they are on the Clean 15 list. If the conventional variety is cheaper, it's fine, get those. Get the big bags of carrots and potatoes, not the individual. Make sure the chicken has no hormones! Get vegetable oil, not expensive olive oil. Get the cheapest spaghetti sauce, I can spruce it up. No chips or fig bars! You have a budget of $150 and NO MORE. Also, get the big blocks of cheese. Find cheap plant-based creamers if you can."

Arjan and Sam love to go grocery shopping. Arjan has learned to read labels since we don't get anything with palm oil to save what we can of the Amazon and rainforests. We don't have to do much label reading anymore because we just buy bulk flour, oil, and produce and whip up everything ourselves. Make it yourself and you get rid of palm oil, dyes, chemicals, and much more.

Arjan also has learned to price compare and to look at weight and price to see where the deal truly is. Sam isn't much help. He throws anything fun looking into the cart when I'm not paying attention. He is great if you want to find new sauces and foods. He loves new foods and delights. He loves to try out new seasonings and sauces. He's very fun that way, but if you are on a budget and trying to stay away from certain things, Arjan is your man.

Now I have a little space and quiet to watch my documentary, finish my coffee, and work. My old dog, Clyde, is sleeping on his bed that I drag out each morning and put in front of the heater so he can sleep in the living room with all of us. Molly is curled up by my legs under our warm throw blanket. I've shut off the main heat and just have a heater in the living room. The baking of the bread warmed the kitchen.

I won't have to cook at all today as I made brown rice, a big pot of pinto beans, a seasoned Cajun-style roast, and homemade tortillas yesterday. This will feed us today and maybe tomorrow. No one complains. The food is flavorful and hearty. We have it in bowls one day, on tortillas another day. We sprinkle a little cheddar and use some sriracha. The trick to leftovers is choosing foods that get better as they sit in the fridge overnight, then changing it a little each day. Chili and cornbread one day. The next day the cornbread is breakfast with butter and jam and the chili is made into chili cheese burritos. Chicken soup and fresh homemade Amish bread one day. The next day the bread is toast for breakfast, and you add dumplings to the chicken soup. The day after that, you thicken up the soup and add more vegetables and make it into a casserole or pot pie. Spaghetti sauce improves with time as well. Spaghetti on pasta one day, lasagna the next day.

Life is good. Truly. I am loving life more each day and when I look in the mirror, I look healthier and younger or more worry-free each day. You can tell a lot from your inner workings by the reflection in the mirror.

I have a T-shirt that says, "I can explain it to you, but I can't *understand* it for you."

I will end this book on that note. I can paint a picture of our life in my writings. I used to do it in my filming of our life. But you must walk this path yourself to feel it and experience it.

We are finally right where I wanted us to be. A cross between the best of modern life and the peaceful and nurturing parts of old-fashioned life. I love my radio, vacuum, and washer, but I no longer have Internet access. Love those lights and heat, but we often choose candlelight in the evenings. I brew my coffee the slow way on purpose, and I walk places when we can, and the weather is nice.

We have withdrawn from the dramas and woes of the world for now, but we still know and care. We do our part in individual ways.

We are very careful with whom we spend our precious time or bring into our home. We have kind and good-hearted friends and we are attracting more like-minded souls all the time. We choose where we go and what we take in carefully as well. It keeps us sane and content in an unhappy world. We remind ourselves that we can't fix others. We can only heal ourselves and then be an example.

We are just starting on this adventure, and I have no idea where we will be in a year or more. Every day, I look at things and make little changes if need be. I find a new way to save on an old bill or cut out something else. I used to have so many things to check on my cell phone but now I have only email and the bank. And neither needs to be checked but once a week. I will not have much data next month and I'm glad for it. I won't be tempted to look things up all the time or watch a YouTube video late at night.

Bali and the boys successfully stayed under $150 for groceries and did find lots of affordable organics. The only points they lost was when they bought me a $6 jar of Better Than Bouillon instead of the $2 powdered chicken bouillon. Live and learn.

I feel like I have so much time now and I do everything I want to do daily without stress. I clean the house, do a short exercise routine, read some, edit my writing, cook, bake...and here I am with the whole evening.

We have been watching a lot of Studio Ghibli movies. These are Japanese stories; some are old folklore and some are a bit more modern. They all have strong messages and make one think about life. The biggest theme in most of these movies is greed and how it destroys us as individuals, destroys Mother Earth and anything good and pure. Greed consumes everything in its path and doesn't stop until it's all gone. The other theme is finding our passion and purpose that give our lives meaning. In *Kiki's Delivery Service* a witch loses her magical powers when she starts working too hard and finds her previous joys in helping others who are diminishing with exhaustion and lack of purpose.

Only Yesterday is about a woman remembering her past and what shaped her presently. It's about her being true to herself in the end. It's more for the grown-up crowd and I highly suggest this one. I cried so hard at the end because it was so happy, but I also had to watch the ending twice to understand what was happening. In the movie, a woman who has an office job in the city spends her summers working on her brother-in-law's family farm. She loves it there. It's beautiful and peaceful, the family adores her, she loves the work, and she meets a man who becomes a good friend and possible romantic situation. She has memories of her fifth-grade self and all the moments that defined her life and shaped who she is today. In the end, the family asks her to stay and marry her friend, Toshio, but she thinks she must go back. I won't spoil the ending, but it is so delightful and joyful, I still cry thinking about it.

I didn't just cry, I wailed and laughed, and cried some more because it is about listening to your inner guidance and doing what brings you joy. So many of us waste our lives doing what we "should be doing" and "being responsible." Well, you can be responsible by doing what brings you fulfillment. That is the most responsible thing you can do for yourself and everyone that must live with you or work with you. If everyone did what they enjoyed, we would have a much happier society and, maybe, less depression and drug abuse.

You may think, "But we need farmworkers and janitors and people to do grunt work!" Guess what? Some people DO love cleaning and farming and doing grunt work, but they also need to find a way to do it that is creative and rich. Even cleaning can be a craft, a skill, and a ritual. The way people are being forced to work and do things is not soul-filling. We need to find other ways to work and serve. That's why so many people started quitting their jobs after the quarantine. They had time to think about life and whether or not they wanted to work this grueling factory life or create something far more interesting.

And that is the question. Can we create something far better for ourselves at work and home? And how do we start right now?

Go ahead and downsize and live on a tight budget for a while and figure it out. I'd rather live on less and forgo the busy life in exchange for having more time to build something meaningful with my family, to be calm and content, not stressed and rushed every day.

By removing all the distractions, I'm focused on what matters. I believe many people are searching for this balance of work and dreams.

This book may seem strange, mixing dreams with budgets. Some may wonder why I talk about stretching a paycheck on the same plate as following your heart. For me, I finally listened to my inner guidance, but I kept stalling because of money worries. Then one day I just started weeding out the things not working or making us happy. I threw it all out and made it work. For us, it meant whittling down the bills to the basics. We have a small budget right now, but I know it's temporary. It hasn't been hard or stressful at all. We are much happier, and life seems brighter, richer, and more colorful than ever.

You only need the basics; everything else you create. Experiences are what make life delicious, not plenty of disposable money.

I hope this book has helped you in some way, even a little bit. Thank you for joining me in my long-winded thoughts and talks. May your life be as well and happy as possible.

Kate

Recommended Books, Movies, and Documentaries

Books

Essentialism, Greg McKeown

What Falls From The Sky, Esther Emery

Evicted: Profit And Poverty In The American City, Matthew Desmond

The Complete Tightwad Gazette, Amy Dacyczyn

Make-A-Mix, Karine Eliason, Nevada Harward, and Madeline Westover

More-Make-A-Mix, Karine Eliason, Nevada Harward, and Madeline Westover

Good and Cheap, Leanne Brown (go on her website to download a free PDF)

Documentaries and Movies

How To Cook Your Life

Spirited Away

Only Yesterday

Walk With Me

Other books by Kate Singh

Home Economics (lots of good recipes)

The Frugal Life

A Sweet Life In Homemaking

The Homemade Housewife

Plus many more! Please visit my author's page on Amazon.